Essent

Revision

Notes

with check-up tests

Key Stage 4
Mathematics
Intermediate Level

Ruso Bradley, June Hall & Mark Haslam

Introduction

This book is aimed at candidates taking the Intermediate tier in GCSE Mathematics, and is suitable for all examination boards.

It's the perfect size to keep with you at all times during the crucial weeks before the exams.

There are concise revision notes for each topic in the four main strands:
- Number
- Algebra
- Shape, space & measures
- Handling data

Everything you need to know about a topic is given on one or two pages, in the same format:
- **Essential facts**
  Everything you need to know, complete with examples.
- **Q & A**
  Easy-to-follow worked examples with clearly explained methods.
- **Check-up TESTs**
  To make sure everything has sunk in.

On pages 86–87 there is a Revision TEST to check that you have remembered all the basic facts.

And if you still don't know what to expect in the exams, get yourself a copy of *Essential Exam Practice* and see.

Good luck in your exams!

Contents

Non-calculator tricks

● **Multiplying by 10, 100, ...**

Move the digits <u>one place left</u> for <u>every zero</u> in 10, 100, ...

● **Dividing by 10, 100, ...**

Move the digits <u>one place right</u> for <u>every zero</u> in 10, 100, ...

➤ **Q & A**

a Multiply 2601.3582 by 100.

b Divide 72.618 by 1000.

Answer

a 260<u>1</u>.3582 ⇒ 260<u>1</u>35.82

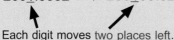

×100

Each digit moves <u>two places left</u>.

Place holders

÷1000

b 72.<u>6</u>18 ⇒ 0.072<u>6</u>18

Each digit moves <u>three places right</u>.

➤ **Method**

❶ <u>Count</u> the number of <u>zeros</u> in 10 or 100 or ...

❷ <u>Move</u> the digits one place left/right <u>for every zero</u>. (Focus on a digit next to the decimal point to help you.)

❸ Use <u>zeros as place holders</u> if necessary.

Use your head.

● **Essential non-calculator tricks**

To <u>add 9</u>, 99, 999, ... <u>add 10</u>, 100, 1000, ... <u>then subtract 1</u>.

To <u>subtract 9</u>, 99, 999, ... <u>subtract 10</u>, 100, 1000, ... <u>then add 1</u>.

To <u>multiply by 9</u>, multiply <u>by 10</u> then subtract the <u>original number</u>.

To <u>multiply by 11</u>, multiply <u>by 10</u> then add the <u>original number</u>.

To <u>multiply by 5</u>, 50, 500, ... <u>multiply by 10</u>, 100, 1000, ... <u>then halve</u>.

To <u>divide by 5</u>, 50, 500, ... <u>divide by 10</u>, 100, 1000, ... <u>then double</u>.

To <u>multiply by 2, 4</u>, 8, ... <u>double, double again</u>, double again, ...

1 Multiply 56 218.13 by **a** 10 **b** 1000 **c** 10 000.

2 Divide 3002.18 by **a** 100 **b** 100 000.

3 Use the 'Essential non-calculator tricks' to do these:

   a 1268 – 99 **b** 380 × 5 **c** 15 × 8 **d** 800 ÷ 500 **e** 280 × 11.

TEST

Special numbers

● Even and odd numbers

Even numbers end in 0, 2, 4, 6 or 8 and are exactly divisible by 2.
All other numbers are odd numbers – they end in 1, 3, 5, 7 or 9.

● Square numbers

Square numbers are whole numbers multiplied by themselves.

> ➤ **Example**
> '3 squared' is 3 × 3 = 9.
> '3 squared' is written 3^2.

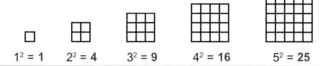

$1^2 = 1$ $2^2 = 4$ $3^2 = 9$ $4^2 = 16$ $5^2 = 25$

● Cube numbers

Cube numbers are whole numbers multiplied by themselves twice.

> ➤ **Example**
> 2 cubed = 2^3 = 2 × 2 × 2 = 8

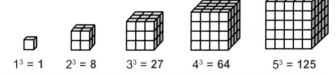

$1^3 = 1$ $2^3 = 8$ $3^3 = 27$ $4^3 = 64$ $5^3 = 125$

● Triangular numbers

Start at 1 and add 2, then 3, then 4, ...

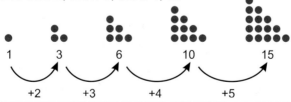

1   3   6   10   15

+2   +3   +4   +5

---

1 Write down the first ten
  a even **b** odd **c** square **d** cube **e** triangular numbers.

2 108, 81, 97, 21, 36, 10, 64
  From the list, write down the
  a even **b** odd **c** square **d** cube **e** triangular numbers.

TEST

5

Number

Powers & roots (1)

● Powers

Powers are just a short way of writing repeated multiplication.

The 'power' or 'index' tells you how many times the number appears in the repeated multiplication.

> **➤ Example**
>
> $5^4 = 5 \times 5 \times 5 \times 5 = 625$
>
> The power is 4, so 5 appears 4 times.
>
> 5^4 is '5 to the power of 4'.

● Special powers

Any non-zero number 'to the power of 0' is 1.

Any number 'to the power of 1' is itself.

> **➤ Examples**
>
> $1^0 = 1,\ 2^0 = 1,\ 9^0 = 1$
>
> $1^1 = 1,\ 2^1 = 2,\ 5^1 = 5$

● Square and cube roots

Finding the root is the opposite (or inverse) of finding the power.

'What is the square root of 16?' means the same as 'What number squared is 16?'

> **➤ Example**
>
> $\sqrt{16} = 4$ or -4
>
> as $4 \times 4 = 16$
>
> and $-4 \times -4 = 16$

➤ Q & A

What is $\sqrt[3]{125}$?

Answer

This is the short way of writing 'What number is the cube root of 125?'

So ask yourself 'What number cubed is 125?'

The answer to this is 5:

$5 \times 5 \times 5 = 125$, so $\sqrt[3]{125} = \underline{5}$

➤ Method

❶ Check whether you are taking the square or cube root.

❷ Ask yourself what number squared/cubed gives the number in the question.

❸ Remember that square roots can be negative.

● Negative powers

A negative power is the reciprocal of a positive power.

('Reciprocal' just means 'one over'.)

> **➤ Examples**
>
> $10^{-3} = \frac{1}{10^3} = \frac{1}{1000} = 0.001$
>
> $6^{-1} = \frac{1}{6^1} = \frac{1}{6}$

Powers & roots (2)

● Working with powers

◆ To <u>multiply powers</u> of the same number <u>add the indices</u>.

◆ To <u>divide powers</u> of the same number <u>subtract the indices</u>.

◆ To take the <u>power of a power</u> <u>multiply the indices</u>.

> **➤ Examples**
>
> $4^2 \times 4^3 = 4^{2+3} = 4^5$
>
> $3^7 \div 3^4 = 3^{7-4} = 3^3$
>
> $(10^2)^6 = 10^{2 \times 6} = 10^{12}$

➤ Q & A   What is $12^9 \div 12^7$?

Answer

$12^9 \div 12^7 = 12^{9-7} = 12^2 = \underline{144}$

> **➤ Method**
>
> ❶ Use the <u>above rules</u> to <u>simplify</u> the calculation.
> ❷ <u>Evaluate</u> the power.

● Fractional powers

These are just another way of showing roots. The <u>denominator</u> (bottom) of the fraction <u>tells you which root</u> to take.

> $25^{\frac{1}{2}} = \sqrt{25} = 5$
>
> $8^{\frac{1}{3}} = \sqrt[3]{8} = 2$

● Powers & roots on your calculator

You should have some buttons like these on your calculator:

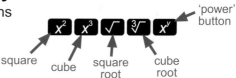

'power' button

square   cube   square root   cube root

To work out $\sqrt{169}$, press [√] [1] [6] [9] [=]. On some calculators you press [√] after you enter the number, i.e. [1] [6] [9] [√].

Sometimes [√] is a '2nd function' written above [x^2]. If your calculator is like this you have to press [SHIFT] [x^2] [1] [6] [9] [=].

To work out 5^8, press [5] [x^y] [8] [=].

---

1 Find these powers: **a** 12^2 **b** 4^3 **c** 2^5 **d** 8^0 **e** 100^1 **f** 10^{-2}

2 Find these roots: **a** $\sqrt{36}$ **b** $\sqrt{64}$ **c** $\sqrt[3]{1000}$ **d** $\sqrt[3]{343}$ **e** $27^{\frac{1}{3}}$

3 Combine these powers: **a** $7^4 \times 7^3$ **b** $2^{10} \div 2^5$ **c** $(5^8)^3$

Check your answers to questions **1** and **2** on your calculator.

TEST

Number

Multiples & factors

● Multiples

The multiples of a number are the numbers in its times table.

➤ Q & A

What are the first five multiples of 14?

Answer

14 × 1 = 14

14 × 2 = 28

14 × 3 = 42

14 × 4 = 56

14 × 5 = 70

If you don't know the 14 times table then you'll have to work it out – just double the 7 times table.

➤ Method

❶ Multiply the number by 1, 2, 3, 4 and 5.

❷ List the answers. These are the first five multiples.

So the first five multiples of 14 are 14, 28, 42, 56 and 70.

● Factors

The factors of a number are the numbers that divide into it exactly (including 1 and itself).

➤ Q & A

List all the factors of 42.

Answer

42 ÷ 1 = 42 ——— Don't forget to divide by 1.

42 ÷ 2 = 21

42 ÷ 3 = 14

42 ÷ 4 = not a whole number

42 ÷ 5 = not a whole number ——— Ignore these.

42 ÷ 6 = 7

42 ÷ 7 = 6 ——— Repeats! Stop here.

➤ Method

❶ Divide by 1, 2, 3, 4, ...

❷ Ignore answers that are not whole numbers.

❸ Stop when you get a repeat.

❹ List all the other numbers that you used.

So the factors of 42 are 1, 2, 3, 6, 7, 14, 21 and 42.

---

1 List the first five multiples of **a** 7 **b** 12 **c** 21 **d** 104.

2 List all the factors of **a** 24 **b** 56 **c** 98.

TEST

LCM & HCF

● Least common multiple

The <u>least common multiple</u> (LCM) is the <u>smallest</u> number that is a <u>multiple</u> of all the numbers in question.

➤ Q & A

What is the LCM of 4 and 14?

Answer

> **➤ Method**
> ❶ List the <u>multiples</u> of both numbers.
> ❷ Pick out the <u>smallest</u> number that's in both lists.

List the multiples of the numbers:
Multiples of 4 are 4, 8, 12, 16, 20, 24, <u>28</u>, 32, ...
Multiples of 14 are 14, <u>28</u>, 42, ...

The smallest number that's in both lists is 28, so <u>28 is the LCM of 4 and 14</u>.

Note: '<u>least</u> common multiple' is the same thing as '<u>lowest</u> common multiple'. Some people prefer lowest, some least – luckily they both shorten to LCM.

● Highest common factor

The <u>highest common factor</u> (HCF) is the <u>largest</u> number that is a <u>factor</u> of all the numbers in question.

➤ Q & A

What is the HCF of 24 and 36?

Answer

> **➤ Method**
> ❶ List the <u>factors</u> of both numbers.
> ❷ Pick out the <u>largest</u> number that's in both lists.

List the factors of the numbers:
Factors of 24 are 1, 2, 3, 4, 6, 8, <u>12</u>, 24
Factors of 36 are 1, 2, 3, 4, 6, 9, <u>12</u>, 18, 36

The largest number that's in both lists is <u>12</u>, so <u>12 is the HCF of 24 and 36</u>.

Write down all your working.

1 What is the LCM of **a** 6 and 8 **b** 16 and 36?
2 What is the HCF of **a** 4 and 16 **b** 21 and 35?

TEST

Number

Prime numbers

● Prime numbers

> A prime number has exactly two factors (itself and 1).

Note: 1 is not a prime number (it has only one factor – itself).

You should memorise the first few primes: 2, 3, 5, 7, 11, 13, 17, ...
(You won't be able to do anything on these two pages if you don't!)

● Is it prime?

To check if a number is prime, all you have to do is divide by primes that are smaller than the square root of the number in question.

➤ Q & A

Is 67 a prime number?

Answer

❶ The square root of 67 is a bit more than 8 (use a calculator or the fact that $8^2 = 64$).

❷ So you only have to divide by 2, 3, 5 and 7.

$67 ÷ 2 =$ not a whole number

$67 ÷ 3 =$ not a whole number

$67 ÷ 5 =$ not a whole number

$67 ÷ 7 =$ not a whole number

➤ Method

❶ Work out the square root of the number.

❷ Divide by all the primes that are smaller than the square root.

❸ If none of them divide into the number exactly, then the number is prime.

❹ If any of them divide into the number exactly, then the number is NOT prime.

❸ None of them divide into it exactly, so 67 is a prime number.

---

1 Work out all the prime numbers less than 50.

2 Are these prime numbers? **a** 2546 **b** 2404 **c** 8765
How could you tell by just looking at the last digits?

3 'A number is divisible by 3 if the sum of its digits is divisible by 3.'
Use this fact to work out whether or not these numbers are prime: **a** 216 **b** 1953 **c** 177 147

TEST

10

Prime factorisation

● Prime factorisation

This means '<u>break a number into its prime factors, and write them multiplied together</u>'.

You'll need to know the first few primes and your times tables.

➤ Q & A

Express 60 as a product of its prime factors.

Answer

60 = 6 × 10 [break into two factors]

= 2 × 3 × 10 [break 6 into 2 × 3]

= 2 × 3 × 2 × 5 [break 10 into 2 × 5]

All the factors are now primes, so you can't break it down any further.

= 2 × 2 × 3 × 5 [rewrite the factors in order of size]

= 2^2 × 3 × 5 [write the answer with indices]

➤ Method

❶ Break the number into <u>pairs of factors</u>.

❷ Continue until all the factors are <u>primes</u>.

❸ Rewrite the prime factors in <u>order of size</u> (smallest first).

❹ If any of the prime factors are <u>repeated</u>, then express them using <u>indices</u>.

➤ Some further examples

170 = 10 × 17 = 2 × 5 × 17

625 = 5 × 125 = 5 × 5 × 25 = 5 × 5 × 5 × 5 = 5^4

396 = 2 × 198 = 2 × 2 × 99 = 2 × 2 × 3 × 33 = 2 × 2 × 3 × 3 × 11

= 2^2 × 3^2 × 11

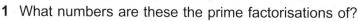

A good plan is to keep dividing by small primes.

---

1 What numbers are these the prime factorisations of?

  a 2 × 3 × 19   **b** 2^2 × 3^2 × 13   **c** 3^3 × 7 × 23

2 Express these numbers as a product of their prime factors:

  a 64   **b** 81   **c** 456   **d** 1225   **e** 2310

Number

Fractions (1)

● Equivalent fractions

You can find <u>equivalent fractions</u> by <u>multiplying/dividing</u> top and bottom by the <u>same number</u>.

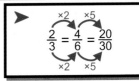

$$\overset{\times 2 \quad \times 5}{\frac{2}{3} = \frac{4}{6} = \frac{20}{30}}_{\times 2 \quad \times 5}$$

● Simplifying fractions

To write a fraction in its simplest form <u>divide</u> <u>numerator and denominator</u> (top and bottom) by the <u>highest common factor</u>.

This is often called '<u>cancelling</u>'.

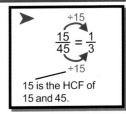

$$\overset{\div 15}{\frac{15}{45} = \frac{1}{3}}_{\div 15}$$

15 is the HCF of 15 and 45.

● Adding/subtracting fractions

You can only add/subtract fraction once they have the <u>same denominators</u>.

➤ Q & A

Work out $\frac{2}{3} + \frac{1}{5}$.

Answer

$\frac{2}{3} + \frac{1}{5}$ [different denominators]

$= \frac{10}{15} + \frac{3}{15}$ [LCM of 3 and 5 is 15]

$= \frac{10 + 3}{15}$ [add numerators]

$= \frac{13}{15}$

➤ Method

❶ <u>Check the denominators</u>. If they are the same go straight to ❸. If not:

❷ Change to fractions with the <u>same denominator</u>. (Use <u>LCM of original denominators</u>.)

❸ Add/subtract <u>numerators</u>.

❹ <u>Simplify</u> if possible.

● Multiplying fractions

Much easier – <u>don't worry about the denominators</u>.

➤ Q & A

Work out $\frac{5}{6} \times \frac{2}{7}$.

Answer

$\frac{5}{6} \times \frac{2}{7} = \frac{5 \times 2}{6 \times 7} = \frac{10}{42} = \frac{5}{21}$

Always simplify your answer

➤ Method

❶ <u>Multiply numerators</u>.

❷ <u>Multiply denominators</u>.

❸ <u>Simplify</u> if possible.

12

Number

Fractions (2)

● Dividing fractions

To divide fractions, you <u>turn the second one over then multiply</u>.

> **Example**

$$\frac{2}{9} \div \frac{3}{7} = \frac{2}{9} \times \frac{7}{3} = \frac{14}{27}$$

(Use the method in the 'Multiplying fractions' **Q & A** on the previous page.)

● Improper & mixed fractions

<u>Improper fractions</u> are 'top heavy', i.e. the numerator is bigger than the denominator.

<u>Mixed numbers</u> are made up of a <u>whole number</u> and a <u>fraction</u>.

> **Examples**

$\frac{8}{5}$ is an improper fraction.

$3\frac{3}{5}$ is a mixed number.

> **Q & A**

Write $2\frac{3}{7}$ as an improper fraction.

Answer

$2\frac{3}{7} = 2 + \frac{3}{7}$

$= \frac{14}{7} + \frac{3}{7}$

$= \frac{17}{7}$

> **Method**

❶ Write the mixed number as the sum of the <u>whole part</u> and the <u>fraction part</u>.
❷ Write the <u>whole number as a fraction with the same denominator</u> as the fraction.
❸ <u>Add</u> the fractions.

> **Q & A**

Write $\frac{18}{5}$ as a mixed number.

Answer

$\frac{18}{5} = \frac{5+5+5+3}{5}$

$= \frac{5}{5} + \frac{5}{5} + \frac{5}{5} + \frac{3}{5}$

$= 3\frac{3}{5}$

> **Method**

❶ Write the numerator as the <u>sum of as many denominators as possible</u>, plus the extra bit.
❷ Write <u>each number over the denominator</u>.
❸ <u>Count</u> the 'whole' fractions.

Work these out. Change any mixed numbers to improper fractions before you start. Give all answers as mixed numbers in their simplest form.

1 a $\frac{3}{4} + \frac{1}{8}$ **b** $\frac{8}{15} - \frac{1}{5}$ **c** $2\frac{1}{3} - 1\frac{1}{4}$

2 a $\frac{5}{12} \times \frac{3}{7}$ **b** $\frac{4}{7} \div \frac{5}{14}$ **c** $1\frac{5}{6} \div \frac{3}{10}$

TEST

13

Number

Fractions (3)

● Converting fractions to decimals

To change a fraction to a decimal you <u>divide the numerator by the denominator</u>.

► Q & A

Convert $\frac{27}{40}$ to a decimal.

Answer

$27 \div 40 = 0.675$

► Method

❶ Write the fraction as a <u>division</u>.
❷ Divide using <u>long division</u> or a <u>calculator</u> if necessary.

● Decimal equivalents you should know

$\frac{1}{2} = 0.5$ $\frac{1}{4} = 0.25$ $\frac{1}{8} = 0.125$ $\frac{1}{5} = 0.2$

$\frac{1}{10} = 0.1$ $\frac{1}{100} = 0.01$ $\frac{1}{3} = 0.333...$ $\frac{2}{3} = 0.666...$

● Fractions on your calculator

Make sure you can do these 6 things with the fraction button 【aᵇ⁄c】.

❶ Press 【2】【aᵇ⁄c】【3】【=】 to enter a proper fraction like $\frac{2}{3}$.

❷ Press 【2】【aᵇ⁄c】【5】【aᵇ⁄c】【6】【=】 for a mixed number like $2\frac{5}{6}$.

❸ Press 【1】【aᵇ⁄c】【4】【+】【2】【aᵇ⁄c】【5】【=】 to work out $\frac{1}{4} + \frac{2}{5}$.

❹ Press 【1】【8】【aᵇ⁄c】【2】【4】【=】 to reduce $\frac{18}{24}$ to its lowest terms.

❺ Press 【SHIFT】【aᵇ⁄c】 to convert between mixed and improper fractions. For example, to convert $2\frac{5}{6}$ press 【2】【aᵇ⁄c】【5】【aᵇ⁄c】【6】【=】 and then 【SHIFT】【aᵇ⁄c】.

❻ Some calculators are so clever that they can convert decimals to fractions. For example, to convert 0.35 to a fraction, press 【0】【●】【3】【5】【=】【aᵇ⁄c】.

(You can convert a fraction to a decimal on any calculator: to convert $\frac{3}{5}$ to a decimal, press 【3】【÷】【5】【=】.)

---

1 Convert these fractions to decimals: **a** $\frac{1}{50}$ **b** $\frac{3}{8}$ **c** $2\frac{17}{25}$

2 Use your calculator to answer the TEST on page 13.

TEST

Fractions, decimals & percentages (1)

● Terminating decimals

Terminating decimals go on for a few decimal places then stop.

You can tell whether a fraction will give a terminating decimal by looking at the denominator. If the only prime factors are 2 and 5, it will terminate. Otherwise it will 'recur' (see below).

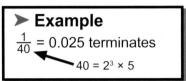

> **Example**
>
> $\frac{1}{40}$ = 0.025 terminates
>
> 40 = $2^3 \times 5$

● Recurring decimals

Recurring decimals have a group of one or more digits that repeat, e.g. 0.333333... and 0.626262... are recurring decimals.

The shorthand way of writing these is to put dots over the first and last digits in the repeating group.

> ➤ $0.\dot{3}$ means 0.333333...
> $0.\dot{6}\dot{2}$ means 0.626262...

● Converting decimals to fractions

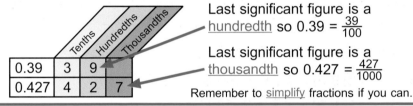

Last significant figure is a hundredth so 0.39 = $\frac{39}{100}$

Last significant figure is a thousandth so 0.427 = $\frac{427}{1000}$

	Tenths	Hundredths	Thousandths
0.39	3	9	
0.427	4	2	7

Remember to simplify fractions if you can.

● Percentages

> 'Per cent' means 'in every 100'.

So '10 per cent' means '10 in every 100'.
The % symbol can be used in place of the words 'per cent'.

● Converting percentages to fractions

Write the percentage as a fraction with denominator 100.
(Don't forget to simplify if you can.)

> **Example**
>
> 54% = $\frac{54}{100}$ = $\frac{27}{50}$

● Converting percentages to decimals

This is pretty simple, just divide by 100.
Remember to get rid of the % symbol.
(See page 4 for the easy way to divide by 100.)

> **Example**
>
> 15% = 15 ÷ 100 = 0.15

Number

Fractions, decimals & percentages (2)

● Converting decimals to percentages

Multiply the decimal by 100%.
(See page 4 for the easy way to multiply by 100.)

> **➤ Example**
> $0.32 = 0.32 \times 100\% = 32\%$

● Converting fractions to percentages

Do this in two steps: fraction → decimal → percentage.

➤ Q & A

Convert $\frac{1}{8}$ to a percentage.

Answer

$\frac{1}{8} = 0.125 = 0.125 \times 100\% = \underline{12.5\%}$

> **➤ Method**
> ❶ Convert to a decimal.
> ❷ Multiply by 100%.

● Ordering fractions, decimals & percentages

➤ Q & A

Order this list, smallest first.

1.3, 115%, 225%, $1\frac{1}{3}$

Answer

1.30, 1.15, 2.25, 1.33...

1.30, 1.15, 1.33..., 2.25

1.15, 1.30, 1.33..., 2.25

115%, 1.3, $1\frac{1}{3}$, 225%

> **➤ Method**
> ❶ Convert any fractions or percentages to decimals.
> ❷ Compare whole numbers. Order the list by these.
> ❸ If several have the same whole number, order these by tenths.
> ❹ Repeat for hundredths, thousandths and so on.
> ❺ Rewrite the list with the original fractions & percentages in place.

---

1 Will the decimal equivalent of $\frac{3}{20}$ terminate?

2 Convert these fractions to recurring decimals. Use the dot notation. **a** $\frac{2}{3}$ **b** $\frac{4}{11}$ **c** $\frac{1}{7}$

3 Write as a fraction: **a** 75% **b** 37.5% **c** 110%

4 Write as a decimal: **a** 55% **b** 17.5% **c** 130%

5 Convert to percentages: **a** 0.75 **b** $\frac{1}{20}$ **c** $1\frac{2}{5}$

6 Order this list, smallest first: 4.6, 135%, 345%, $3\frac{1}{4}$

TEST

Percentages (1)

Most percentage problems can solved by first <u>finding the value of 1%</u>.

● **Percentage of**

➤ Q & A
Find 20% of £400.

Answer

1% is £400 ÷ 100 = £4

20% is £4 × 20 = £80

➤ **Method**
❶ <u>Divide</u> by 100 <u>to find 1%</u>.
❷ <u>Multiply</u> by the number of per cent required.

● **Percentage increase/decrease**

➤ Q & A
A game costs £20 plus VAT. If VAT is 17.5%, how much does the game cost?

Answer

1% of £20 is £20 ÷ 100 = £0.20.

➤ **Method**
❶ Find the <u>increase</u> (or decrease).
❷ <u>Add it</u> to the price. (<u>Take it off</u> for a decrease.)

VAT is 17.5% of £20, which is £0.20 × 17.5 = £3.50 (this is the <u>increase</u>).

The game costs £20 + £3.50 = <u>£23.50</u>.

● **Finding the price before a percentage decrease**
Always think of the <u>original price as 100%</u> and work out what percentage the price you're given is. (It will be less than 100%.)

➤ Q & A
In a sale, all items are reduced by 25%. If a coat costs £37.50 in the sale, how much did it cost originally?

Answer Think of the <u>original price</u> as 100%. The <u>cost now</u> is 100% − 25% = 75%.

So 75% is £37.50

Then 1% is £37.50 ÷ 75 = £0.50

Therefore 100% is £0.50 × 100 = <u>£50</u>

➤ **Method**
❶ Work out <u>what percentage</u> the price is <u>now</u>.
❷ <u>Divide</u> the price by this percentage <u>to find 1%</u>.
❸ <u>Multiply by 100</u> to find the original price.

Number

Percentages (2)

● Finding the price before a percentage increase
You use the <u>same method</u>, but the price now is more than 100%.

➤ Q & A
A bike costs £470 including VAT.
What was the price before VAT
was added?

Answer
Think of the price <u>before</u> VAT as 100%.
Price <u>including</u> VAT is 100% + 17.5% = 117.5%.
So 117.5% is £470
Then 1% is £470 ÷ 117.5 = £4
Therefore 100% is £4 × 100 = <u>£400</u>

➤ Method
❶ Work out <u>what</u>
   <u>percentage</u> the price
   is <u>now</u>.
❷ <u>Divide</u> the price by
   this percentage <u>to</u>
   <u>find 1%</u>.
❸ <u>Multiply by 100</u> to
   find the original price.

● Percentage change   (You don't have to find 1% first for this sort.)

$$\text{Percentage change} = \frac{\text{Actual change}}{\text{Original quantity}} \times 100\%$$

➤ Q & A
Dave bought a football for £32.
He then sold it for £36.
What was the percentage
change in price?

➤ Method
❶ Work out the <u>actual change</u>
   and <u>original quantity</u>.
❷ Use the <u>formula</u> to work out
   the <u>percentage change</u>.

Answer
Actual change = £36 – £32 = £4   Original price = £32
So percentage change = $\frac{4}{32}$ × 100% = <u>12.5%</u>
With money, percentage change is called percentage profit or loss; this was a 12.5% profit.

---

1 a What is 15% of 250 g?   **b** Decrease 250 g by 15%.
2 A jumper is reduced by 10% to £18.
    What was the price before the reduction?
3 The cost including VAT is £94. Take off the VAT (at 17.5%).
4 Lauren bought an electronic keyboard for £112, then sold it
    for £98. What was the percentage loss?

TEST

Percentages (3)

● Compound interest

(See next page for TEST)

➤ Q & A

£500 was invested for 3 years. Compound interest of 4% was paid annually.

What is the investment now worth?

Answer

➤ Method

❶ Work out the <u>interest for year 1</u>.
❷ Find the <u>total value after 1 year</u>.
❸ <u>Repeat</u> for the other years, always working out the interest on the <u>previous year's total value</u>.

Year	Interest	Total Value
1	4% of £500 = £20	£500 + £20 = £520
2	4% of £520 = £20.80	£520 + £20.80 = £540.80
3	4% of £540.80 = £21.63	£540.80 + £21.63 = <u>£562.43</u>

Ratio & proportion (1)

<u>Ratios compare quantities</u>, like the amounts of fat and flour in pastry.

> ➤ 50 g fat to 100 g flour is written 50 : 100.

● Simplifying ratios

<u>Multiplying/dividing both sides</u> of a ratio by any number gives an <u>equivalent ratio</u>.

The <u>simplest form</u> has both amounts as <u>whole numbers</u>, with <u>no common factors</u>.

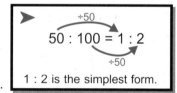

> ➤
> ÷50
> 50 : 100 = 1 : 2
> ÷50
>
> 1 : 2 is the simplest form.

➤ Q & A

It is 1.75 km to the shop and 2.5 km to the library.

What is the ratio of the distances?

Answer

1.75 : 2.5 [already in same units]

175 : 250 [×100]

<u>7 : 10</u> [÷25]

➤ Method

❶ Write the amounts in the <u>same units</u>.
❷ Write the two amounts <u>without units</u> as '<u>amount : amount</u>'.
❸ <u>If necessary</u>, multiply both sides by <u>any big number</u> to get rid of decimals/fractions.
❹ <u>Divide by the HCF</u> to simplify.

Number

Ratio & proportion (2)

● Dividing in a given ratio

➤ Q & A

Divide £120 in the ratio 2 : 3.

Answer

2 + 3 = 5 parts
1 part is £120 ÷ 5 = £24
2 parts are £24 × 2 = £48
3 parts are £24 × 3 = £72

£48 : £72

➤ Method

❶ Add the ratio to find the total number of parts.
❷ Find the value of 1 part.
❸ Multiply by the number of parts on each side of the ratio.

● Proportion

Quantities are in direct proportion if their ratio stays the same however much you have. For example, the ratio of fat to flour in pastry is always the same, no matter how many pies you make.

➤ Q & A

I put 26 litres of petrol in my car and it costs £19.76.

How much would 5 litres cost?

Answer

26 litres : £19.76
1 litre : £0.76   [÷26]
5 litres : £3.80   [×5]

5 litres costs £3.80.

➤ Method

❶ Write down the ratio.
❷ Divide by the number of 'things' you're interested in (litres in this case).
❸ Multiply by the number of 'things' you want.

---

1 Simplify: **a** 3 : 18   **b** 27 : 15   **c** $\frac{3}{8}$: 1

2 175 red cars and 215 blue. What is the ratio of red to blue?

3 Divide 800 ml in the ratio 3 : 7.

4 8 notebooks cost £3.60. How much will 15 cost?

TEST

Percentages (page 19)

A house was valued at £50 000 three years ago. If house prices have risen 12% per year, how much is it worth now?

TEST

20

Negative numbers

● Multiplying and dividing

Remember these rules for multiplying or dividing negative numbers.

❶ If the <u>signs are the same</u>, the answer is <u>positive</u> (+ + or − − is +).

❷ If the <u>signs are different</u>, the answer is <u>negative</u> (+ − or + − is −).

> ### ➤ Examples
>
> The signs are the <u>same</u>: $+6 \times +2 = +12$ $+6 \div +2 = +3$
>
> $-6 \times -2 = +12$ $-6 \div -2 = +3$
>
> The signs are <u>different</u>: $-6 \times +2 = -12$ $-6 \div +2 = -3$
>
> $+6 \times -2 = -12$ $+6 \div -2 = -3$

● Adding and subtracting

Use a <u>number line</u> to help you <u>add or subtract negative numbers</u>.

➤ Q & A   What is $3 - 7$?

Answer

Start at 3 and count back 7 places, giving an answer of <u>−4</u>.

➤ Q & A   What is $-3 - (-8)$?

Answer

First of all deal with the 'minus minus'; together they make a plus.

So $-3 - (-8) = -3 + 8$

Start at −3 and count forward 8 places, giving an answer of <u>5</u>.

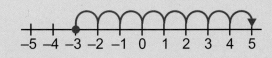

● The sign change button

Your calculator will have a button like one of these: **+/−** **(−)**.
Make sure you know how to <u>enter negative numbers</u> with it.

Work these out and then check your answers using a calculator.

a $24 \div -6$ **b** -5×-6 **c** -12×12

d $3 - 6$ **e** $-14 - 12$ **f** $-34 - (-54)$

TEST

Number

Rounding (1)

● Rounding to the nearest ten

❶ Focus on the <u>tens digit</u>.

37<u>2</u>1.6 ⇒ 372<u>0</u>

❷ If the number to the <u>right</u> of the <u>tens digit</u> (i.e. the units) is <u>5 or more, round up</u>. Otherwise the tens digit <u>stays the same</u>.

❸ <u>Get rid of</u> everything to the <u>right</u> of the tens column. Remember to put a <u>zero as a place holder</u> in the units column.

● Rounding to the nearest hundred, thousand, ...

Do this the same way as rounding to the nearest ten, but <u>focus on the hundreds or thousands</u> digit.

> **Example**
> 3721.6 → 3700 to nearest 100
> 3721.6 → 4000 to nearest 1000

● Rounding to decimal places

'<u>Decimal place</u>' is often abbreviated to '<u>dp</u>' or '<u>d.p.</u>'.

When rounding to <u>1 dp</u> focus on the <u>1st</u> digit after the decimal point. For <u>2 dp</u>, <u>3 dp</u>, ... focus on the <u>2nd</u>, <u>3rd</u>, ... digit after the decimal point.

> **Q & A**

Round 0.168 to 2 dp.

Answer

Focus on the 2nd decimal place.

0.16<u>8</u> ⇒ 0.17

8 is '5 or more', so round 6 <u>up</u> to 7.

> **Method** (rounding to 2 dp)
> ❶ Focus on the 2nd dp.
> ❷ If the digit to the <u>right</u> of the 2nd dp is <u>5 or more, round upwards</u>. Otherwise the 2nd dp <u>stays the same</u>.
> ❸ <u>Get rid</u> of everything to the <u>right</u> of the 2nd dp.

Rounding (2)

● Rounding to significant figures

The 1st significant figure is the 1st non-zero digit from the left.

The 2nd, 3rd, ... significant figures are the digits immediately after the 1st significant figure, even if they are zeros.

'Significant figures' is often shortened to 'sig figs', 'sig. figs.', 'sf' or 's.f.'.

> ### ➤ Example

	1st	2nd	3rd	4th
0 . 0	5	0	9	6

> ### ➤ Q & A

Round 5384 to 2 sig figs.

Answer

Focus on the 2nd sig fig.

5384 ⟶ 5400

8 is '5 or more', so round upwards.

Add zeros. (It would be silly to round to 54.)

> ### ➤ Method (rounding to 2 sf)
>
> ❶ Focus on the 2nd sig fig.
> ❷ If the digit to the right of the 2nd sig fig is 5 or more, round upwards. Otherwise it stays the same.
> ❸ Get rid of everything to the right of the 2nd sig fig. (Add zeros as place holders if needed.)

● Some extra rounding examples

Make sure you can see how these were rounded.

	to 1 dp	to 2 dp	to 3 dp	to 1 sf	to 2 sf	to 3 sf
24.9374	24.9	24.94	24.937	20	25	24.9
0.9527	1.0	0.95	0.953	1	0.95	0.953
0.07457	0.1	0.07	0.075	0.07	0.075	0.0746
888.8888	888.9	888.89	888.889	900	890	889

1 Round these to the nearest hundred: 27 920, 2875, 62
2 Round these to 2 dp: 0.582, 0.019, 12.882
3 Round these to 2 sf: 352, 1.006, 0.809
4 Estimate the answer to these by first rounding all numbers to 1 sf: **a** $\dfrac{(5.45 + 10.85)}{2.86}$ **b** $\dfrac{(989 \times 304)}{296}$

TEST

Number

Standard index form (1)

● Writing numbers in standard index form

Standard index form (sometimes just called standard form) is a short way of writing really small or large numbers.

A number written in standard form is always 'something times 10 to the power of something':

The first number is always a number between 1 and 10. (It can be 1 but not 10.)

$$3 \times 10^9$$

The power of 10 tells you how far the decimal point has moved.

Written the long way, this number is 3 000 000 000.

➤ Q & A

Write 36 000 in standard form.

Answer

The decimal point needs to move 4 places to get to a number between 1 and 10:

 $3\!\cdot\!6000\!\cdot$

36 000 is greater than 1, so the power of 10 is positive.

So, in standard form, the number is written as 3.6×10^4.

➤ Method

❶ Move the decimal point until the number is between 1 and 10.

❷ The power of 10 is the number of places the decimal point moved.

❸ If the original number was greater than 1 then the power is positive.

❹ If the original number was smaller than 1 then the power is negative.

➤ Q & A

Write 0.0045 in standard form.

Answer

The decimal point needs to move 3 places to get to a number between 1 and 10:

 $0\!\cdot\!004\!\cdot\!5$

0.0045 is less than 1, so the power of 10 is negative.

So, in standard form, the number is written as 4.5×10^{-3}.

Write these numbers in standard index form.

a 345   b 0.000 24   c 45 000

d 764 000 000   e 0.000 002 453   f 10 million

TEST

Standard index form (2)

● Changing back to normal numbers

➤ Q & A
Write 2.3×10^{-5} as a normal number.

Answer
The power of 10 is negative so we are dealing with a number less than 1, and the decimal point needs to move 5 places to the left:

Put extra zeros in ➤ 0.00002.3

So the answer is <u>0.000 023</u>.

➤ Method
Move the decimal point the <u>number of places</u> indicated by the <u>power</u> of 10.

Remember, <u>negative powers</u> mean that the number is <u>less than 1</u>.

● Multiplying or dividing

➤ Q & A
Work out $(6 \times 10^5) \times (2 \times 10^4)$.

Answer
$(6 \times 10^5) \times (2 \times 10^4)$
$= (6 \times 2) \times (10^5 \times 10^4)$
$= 12 \times 10^{5+4}$
$= 12 \times 10^9$
$= \underline{1.2 \times 10^{10}}$

➤ Q & A
Work out $(8 \times 10^7) \div (2 \times 10^3)$.

Answer
$(8 \times 10^7) \div (2 \times 10^3)$
$= (8 \div 2) \times (10^7 \div 10^3)$
$= 4 \times 10^{7-3}$
$= \underline{4 \times 10^4}$

➤ Method
❶ Rewrite with the <u>'numbers between 1 and 10'</u> at the <u>front</u> and the <u>'powers of 10'</u> together at the <u>end</u>.
❷ <u>Multiply/divide</u> the numbers in the new groups.
❸ Give the <u>answer</u> in <u>standard form</u> (unless asked not to).

See page 7 if you don't know how to multiply or divide powers.

Write these as normal numbers.

a 3.7×10^3 **b** 4.4×10^{-4} **c** 5.43×10^6 **d** 1.2×10^{-6}

TEST

Standard index form (3)

● Adding or subtracting

➤ Q & A
Work out $(2.5 \times 10^5) + (3.4 \times 10^4)$.

Answer
$(2.5 \times 10^5) + (3.4 \times 10^4)$
$= 250\,000 + 34\,000$
$= 284\,000$
$= \underline{2.84 \times 10^5}$

> ➤ **Method**
> ❶ Change the numbers to normal numbers.
> ❷ Add or subtract the numbers.
> ❸ Give the answer in standard form (unless asked not to).

● Standard index form with a calculator

Your calculator will have a button that looks like one of these:
EXP **E** **EE** **×10ˣ**. This is the standard form button.

To enter a standard form number like 4.6×10^{11} into your calculator just press **4** **●** **6** **EXP** **1** **1** **=** and you'll get something like │ 4.6 ¹¹ │ on your display.

➤ Q & A
Use your calculator to work out $(4 \times 10^9) + (5 \times 10^{10})$.

Answer
Press **4** **EXP** **9** **+** **5** **EXP** **1** **0** **=**
and you'll get │ 5.4 ¹⁰ │. This means the answer is $\underline{5.4 \times 10^{10}}$.
(Do not write 5.4^{10}, that means something else!)

---

1 Give your answers to these in standard index form.
  a $(5 \times 10^5) \times (4 \times 10^4)$ b $(4.1 \times 10^3) \times (2 \times 10^4)$
  c $(8 \times 10^9) \div (4 \times 10^6)$ d $(1.4 \times 10^{-2}) \div (7 \times 10^{-4})$
  e $(2 \times 10^5) + (4 \times 10^4)$ f $(6.4 \times 10^3) + (7 \times 10^4)$
  g $(8 \times 10^{-3}) - (4 \times 10^{-3})$ h $(8.2 \times 10^7) - (7 \times 10^5)$
2 Check your answers to Q1 on your calculator.

TEST

BIDMAS & bracket buttons

● BIDMAS

Always do operations in this order:

Brackets, Indices, Divide and Multiply, Add and Subtract

➤ Q & A

What is $3 + 2 \times (4 - 1)^2$?

Answer

$3 + 2 \times (4 - 1)^2$

$= 3 + 2 \times 3^2$

$= 3 + 2 \times 9$

$= 3 + 18 = \underline{21}$

➤ Method

❶ Do calculations inside brackets first.

❷ Then work out indices, i.e. square, cube, etc.

❸ Divide and multiply.

❹ Finally, add and subtract.

● The bracket buttons (and BIDMAS)

Use the bracket buttons, **[(** **)]**, on your calculator to make sure that it works things out in the correct order. Look at this example:

If you want to work out $\frac{34 - 10}{5 + 2}$ you'll get the wrong answer if you press **[3] [4] [−] [1] [0] [÷] [5] [+] [2] [=]**.

This is because calculators use BIDMAS (see above) to work things out. Here a calculator would first work out the division $(10 \div 5)$, then the addition and subtraction.

To get the correct answer you have to use brackets:

[(] [3] [4] [−] [1] [0] [)] [÷] [(] [5] [+] [2] [)] [=]

● Some other very useful calculator buttons

Make sure you know how to use these important buttons on your calculator.

◀ ▶	These move the curser back and forward along the display.
DEL	It deletes the character where the curser is. Use it with **◀ ▶**.
SHIFT 2nd INV	These let you use functions written above buttons, such as $\tan^{-1}$.

Work these out on paper using BIDMAS. Check your answers using the bracket buttons on your calculator:

a $(3 + 6)(56 - 34)$ **b** $(15 - 2)^2$ **c** $\frac{34 - 24}{6 + 8}$ **d** $\frac{64 \times 44}{128 \div 8}$

TEST

Section 2 – Algebra

Section 2 – Algebra

Using letters

● Don't run before you can walk...

Most people say they hate algebra, perhaps you do too. But really there's <u>no need to panic</u> – you just have to master <u>one</u> topic at a time. (If you can't do the TEST at the end of a topic then you haven't <u>mastered</u> it!)

● Terms, expressions, equations & formulae

A <u>term</u> is some letters and numbers multiplied (or divided) together, e.g x, $4x$, $8x^2$, $2xy$, 14, $\frac{x}{y}$ and $\frac{x-4}{3}$ are all terms.

An <u>expression</u> is a set of terms added (or subtracted) together, e.g. $4x + 8x^2 - 14$ is an expression.

An <u>equation</u> shows that two expressions are <u>equal</u>, e.g. $x + 2 = 3x$.

A <u>formula</u> is a rule for <u>calculating values</u>, e.g. A can be calculated from B using the formula $A = B + 3$.

● Writing formulae

➤ Q & A

A plumber charges £20 to come out, plus £15 for every hour worked. Write a formula for the total cost, C, for a job taking t hours.

Answer

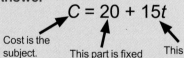

$$C = 20 + 15t$$

Cost is the subject.

This part is fixed – you always have to pay £20.

This part is variable – it depends how long the job takes.

➤ Method

❶ Write down '<u>subject =</u>'. (The subject is the thing the formula will be used to calculate.)

❷ Start the formula with the <u>fixed</u> part.

❸ Finish with the <u>variable</u> part.

1 Are these terms, expressions, equations or formulae?
   a $4x$ **b** $18c + 19d$ **c** $T = 9p + q$ **d** $x^2 + 4x - 3 = 0$

2 Rik buys p pens costing £1.50 each.
   a Write an expression for the cost of the pens.

   Rik pays with a £10 note.
   b Write a formula for the amount of change (C) he receives.

TEST

28

Algebra

Substituting values

● Putting a number into a formula

In the **Q & A** on the previous page you found a formula for the cost (C) of hiring a plumber for t hours: $C = 20 + 15t$.

You can now substitute a number for t and find the cost.

➤ Q & A

Use the formula $C = 20 + 15t$ to find the cost of hiring a plumber for 6 hours.

Answer

$C = 20 + 15t$ Put 6 in place
               of t in the
$C = 20 + 15 × 6$ formula.

$C = 20 + 90$

$C = 110$

So the cost of hiring a plumber for 6 hours is £110.

➤ Method

❶ Write out the formula.
❷ Write it out again with the number in place of the letter.
❸ Use BIDMAS to calculate the value.

● Putting more than one number into a formula

➤ Q & A

Find the value of $v = u + at$ when $u = 4$, $a = -3$ and $t = 5$.

Answer

$v = u + at$

$v = 4 + -3 × 5$

$v = 4 + -15$ Do BIDMAS a step
              at a time, just in
$v = 4 - 15$ case you make a
$v = -11$ mistake.

➤ Method

❶ Write out the formula.
❷ Write it out again with the numbers in place of the letters.
❸ Use BIDMAS to calculate the value.

---

1 What is the cost of hiring a plumber for 20 hours? ($C = 20 + 15t$)
2 Find the value of $v = u + at$ when
   a $u = 7$, $a = 2$, $t = 3$ **b** $u = 0$, $a = -2$, $t = 8$
3 Find the value of $C = \frac{5}{9}(F - 32)$ when
   a $F = 59$ **b** $F = 86$ **c** $F = 77$

TEST

Algebra

Simplifying expressions (1)

● Collecting like terms

'Like terms' are parts of expressions that are similar:

- ◆ x, $5x$ and $18x$ are like terms (they all have an 'x')
- ◆ 1, 345, −34 are like terms (they are all just numbers)
- ◆ xy^2, $14xy^2$, $122xy^2$ are like terms (they all have an 'xy^2')

➤ Q & A

Simplify this expression by collecting like terms:

$8x + 5y − 5x + 4 + 3x + 2y − 12$

Answer

$8x + 5y − 5x + 4 + 3x + 2y − 12$

$= 8x − 5x + 3x + 5y + 2y + 4 − 12$

$= 6x + 7y − 8$

➤ Method

❶ Group 'like terms' together.

❷ Combine 'like terms' by adding or subtracting them.

Group x-terms first, then y-terms then numbers.

● Simplifying expressions with brackets

The term in front of a bracket multiplies everything inside it.

➤ Q & A

Expand the brackets and then collect like terms:

$5(a + 2b) − 4(b + c)$

Answer

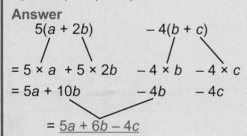

$5(a + 2b) \qquad − 4(b + c)$

$= 5 × a + 5 × 2b \qquad − 4 × b \quad − 4 × c$

$= 5a + 10b \qquad\qquad − 4b \qquad − 4c$

$= 5a + 6b − 4c$

➤ Method

❶ Expand brackets. Remember to subtract every term if you are subtracting a bracket.

❷ Collect like terms.

---

1 Simplify: **a** $4a + 6a − 4a$ **b** $x^2 + 4x + 2x^2 − 6x + 7x$

2 Expand brackets then simplify.

a $7(x − 3y) + 2(x + y)$ **b** $p(5p + 2) − 4(p^2 + p − 1)$

TEST

30

Simplifying expressions (2)

● Multiplying out double brackets

➤ Q & A

Simplify $(2a + 3)(a - 2)$.

Answer

It doesn't need to be a work of art – just join each term in the first bracket to each term in the second.

$= (2a \times a) + (2a \times -2) + (3 \times a) + (3 \times -2)$

Left eyebrow　　Mouth　　　　Nose　　Right eyebrow

$= 2a^2 - 4a + 3a - 6$

$= 2a^2 - a - 6$

➤ Method

❶ Draw a face with two eyebrows, a nose and a mouth:

❷ Multiply together the terms that are joined by lines.

❸ Collect like terms together.

Factorising expressions

● Factorising

Factorising means putting brackets in.

➤ Q & A

Factorise $20x^2 - 15x$.

Answer

$20x^2 - 15x$

$= 5(4x^2 - 3x)$　　5 is a factor, so take it out.

$= 5x(4x - 3)$　　x is also a factor, so take it out too.

Not sure what a factor is? It is something that divides exactly into all the terms.

➤ Method

❶ Look for a common factor. Take this outside the bracket.

❷ Look again. If you can see another factor take it outside the bracket too.

❸ Repeat until no factors are left.

1　Simplify:　**a** $(x + 4)(x + 5)$　**b** $(x - 3)(2x + 2)$　**c** $(2y - 6)(2y - 3)$

2　Factorise:　**a** $6y - 2$　**b** $10p + 5$　**c** $rs + r$

3　Factorise:　**a** $18y^2 - 4y$　**b** $p^3 + p^2$　**c** $12r^2s + 3rs - 4s$

4　Simplify this fraction by first factorising the numerator and denominator, then cancelling.　$\dfrac{5x^2 - 20x}{x^3 - 4x^2}$

TEST

Algebra

Rearranging formulae

Making x the <u>subject</u> of a <u>formula</u> means rewriting it as <u>$x = \dots$</u>
The formula often has a power of the subject or the subject occurs twice.

● What to do with powers of the subject

➤ Q & A

Make x the subject of $y = 36x^2$.

Answer

$y = 36x^2$

$\sqrt{y} = 6x$ [square root]

$\dfrac{\sqrt{y}}{6} = x$ [÷6]

$x = \dfrac{\sqrt{y}}{6}$ [rewrite]

➤ Method

❶ If the <u>subject</u> has been squared, <u>square root both sides</u> of the equation. If the subject has been cubed, take the cube root.

❷ <u>Divide both sides</u> by the number now multiplying the subject.

❸ Rewrite the equation with the <u>subject on the left</u>.

● What to do if the subject occurs twice

➤ Q & A

Make x the subject of
$x + 6 = 3x + y$.

Answer

$x + 6 = 3x + y$

$6 = 2x + y$ [−x]

$2x + y = 6$ [rewrite]

$2x = 6 - y$ [+y]

$x = \dfrac{6 - y}{2}$ [÷2]

➤ Method

❶ Subtract the <u>smallest</u> subject term from both sides.

❷ <u>Rewrite</u> the equation with the remaining <u>subject</u> term <u>on the left</u> if necessary.

❸ <u>Add/subtract</u> any <u>non-subject terms</u> on the left to/from both sides.

❹ <u>Divide both sides</u> by the number now multiplying the subject.

---

1 Make q the subject of   **a** $p = 4q^2$ **b** $p = 81q^2$

2 Make a the subject of   **a** $2a + 3b = a + 1$ **b** $a + 5b = 4a - b$

TEST

Solving equations

● Solving linear equations without brackets

Remember: Whatever you do to one side you must do to the other.

➤ Q & A (1)

Solve $7x - 4 = x + 2$.

Answer

$$7x - 4 = x + 2$$
$$6x - 4 = 2 \qquad [-x]$$
$$6x = 6 \qquad [+4]$$
$$x = 1 \qquad [\div 6]$$

➤ Method

❶ Get rid of the <u>smallest x-term</u>. x is now on one side only.
❷ <u>Add/subtract</u> any <u>numbers</u> on the x-side to/from both sides.
❸ <u>Divide both sides</u> by the number multiplying x.

● Equations with brackets and fractions

➤ Q & A (2)

Solve $6(3y - 2) = 3(3y + 5)$.

Answer

$6 \times 3y - 6 \times 2 = 3 \times 3y + 3 \times 5$ [expand brackets]

$18y - 12 = 9y + 15$

You can now solve this using the first method (see TEST Q2).

➤ Method

❶ <u>Expand</u> the <u>brackets</u>.
❷ Solve as above.

➤ Q & A (3)

Solve $\frac{p-3}{2} = \frac{2p+1}{3}$.

Answer

$$\frac{p-3}{2} \times 6 = \frac{2p+1}{3} \times 6 \qquad [\times 6]$$

$$3(p - 3) = 2(2p + 1)$$

$$3p - 9 = 4p + 2 \qquad \text{[expand brackets]}$$

You can now solve this using the first method (see TEST Q3).

➤ Method

❶ <u>Multiply both sides</u> by the <u>LCM</u> of the <u>denominators</u>.
❷ <u>Expand</u> the <u>brackets</u>.
❸ Solve as above.

1 Solve $5g + 3 = 2g + 6$.   **2** Finish **Q & A (2)**.

3 Finish **Q & A (3)**.

4 Solve: **a** $2(13 - m) = m + 2$ **b** $\frac{n}{2} = \frac{n+4}{4}$

TEST

Algebra

Straight line graphs (1)

● Plotting a straight line with a table of values

➤ Q & A

Draw the graph of $y = 2x + 2$ by first constructing a table of values.

Answer

x	−2	−1	0	1	2
$y = 2x + 2$	−2	0	2	4	6

$2 \times (-2) + 2$

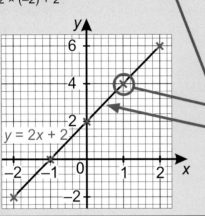

$y = 2x + 2$

➤ Method

❶ Draw a table with an '$\underline{x}$' row and a '$\underline{y}$' row.

❷ Put at least three numbers in the '$\underline{x}$' row.

❸ Work out the corresponding values in the '$\underline{y}$' row.

❹ Plot the pairs of values on graph paper.

❺ Draw a straight line through the points.

This pair of values gives the point (1, 4). (1, 4) is plotted here.

Use a ruler to draw the straight line.

● Gradient

$$\text{Gradient} = \frac{\text{vertical change}}{\text{horizontal change}}$$

$$= \frac{\text{change in } y}{\text{change in } x}$$

Just pick two points on the line, then divide the vertical change by the horizontal change.

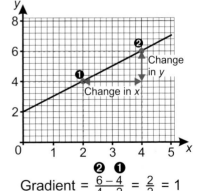

Change in y

Change in x

$$\text{Gradient} = \frac{6-4}{4-2} = \frac{2}{2} = 1$$

● Positive or negative gradient?

If the graph slopes upwards (╱) the gradient will be positive.

If the graph slopes downwards (╲) the gradient will be negative.

34

Straight line graphs (2)

● $y = mx + c$

m is the gradient. The greater the value of m the steeper the graph.

c is the y-intercept. This tells you the graph cuts the y-axis at (0, c).

➤ Q & A

Find the equation of this straight line.

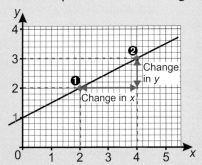

➤ **Method**
1. Work out m (the gradient).
2. Find c (where the line cuts the y-axis).
3. Pop the values of m and c into the equation $y = mx + c$.

Answer

First work out m, the gradient.

$$m = \frac{\text{change in } y}{\text{change in } x} = \frac{3-2}{4-2} = \frac{1}{2}$$

The gradient is positive as the line slopes upwards.

The graph cuts the y-axis at (0, 1), so $c = 1$.

This gives the equation $y = \frac{1}{2}x + 1$.

---

1. By first constructing a table of values from $x = -2$ to $x = 3$, plot the graph of $y = 3x - 4$.

   Where does the graph cross the x-axis?

2. State the gradient of each line and where it crosses the y-axis.
   a $y = 3x + 5$
   b $y = 2x - 1$

3. Work out the equations of the lines below.

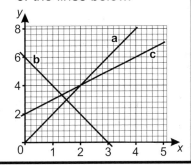

TEST

35

Simultaneous equations (1)

● Solving simultaneous equations graphically

<u>Simultaneous equations</u> are equations that are <u>both true at the same time</u> so you have to <u>solve them both at the same time</u>.

You can plot the graphs of the equations and read off the solution.

➤ **Q & A**

Solve graphically:

$y = x + 2$

$y = 4 - x$

Answer

➤ **Method**

❶ Draw a <u>table of values</u>.
❷ <u>Plot</u> the graphs.
❸ Read off the <u>x- and y-values</u> where the graphs <u>cross</u>.

You only need two points to draw a straight line, but <u>plot three in case you make a mistake</u>.

x	−2	0	2
y = x + 2	0	2	4
y = 4 − x	6	4	2

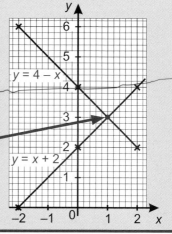

The graphs cross at (1, 3) so the solution is:

<u>x = 1 and y = 3</u>

● There is no excuse for getting it wrong!

You should get these right every time, because you can <u>check your answer</u> – just pop the values from your answer back into the <u>original equations</u> to see if they work.

(Check the **Q & A** above by putting $x = 1$, $y = 3$ into $y = x + 2$ and $y = 4 - x$.)

TEST

1 Solve graphically:
   $y = x - 3$
   $y = 9 - 2x$

2 Solve graphically:
   $y = -x$
   $y = 3x - 4$

3 Why do $y = 2x + 3$ and $y = 2x - 1$ have no solution?

Simultaneous equations (2)

● Solving simultaneous equations algebraically

You don't have to draw a graph to solve simultaneous equations – you can solve them algebraically. Just remember that you're looking for <u>values of the two variables</u> (usually x and y) that <u>work in both equations</u>.

➤ Q & A

Solve algebraically:

$y = 6x - 16$

$2x + 3y = 12$

Answer

A	$-6x +$	y	$= -16$	$[-6x]$
B	$2x + 3y$		$= 12$	$[OK]$
C	$-6x +$	y	$= -16$	
D	$6x + 9y$		$= 36$	$[\times 3]$
		$10y$	$= 20$	$[\textbf{C} + \textbf{D}]$
		y	$= 2$	$[\div 10]$

$2x +$	6	$= 12$	$[put\ y = 2\ into\ \textbf{B}]$
	$2x$	$= 6$	$[-6]$
	x	$= 3$	$[\div 2]$

So the solution is $\underline{x = 3\ and\ y = 2}$.

➤ Method

❶ <u>Rewrite</u> both equations as $ax + by = c$. Label **A** and **B**.

❷ <u>Multiply</u> one (or both) of the equations by something to <u>get the same number in front of x (or y)</u> in both equations. Label **C** and **D**.

❸ <u>Add/subtract</u> one equation to/from the other to <u>eliminate x or y</u>.

❹ <u>Solve</u> this equation.

❺ <u>Substitute</u> this value into one of the <u>original</u> equations.

❻ <u>Solve</u> this equation.

❼ <u>Check</u> your answer.

Check the answer by putting the $x = 3$ and $y = 2$ back into the original equations:

$y = 6x - 16$  $(6 \times 3) - 16 = 2$ ✓

$2x + 3y = 12$ ➧ $(2 \times 3) + (3 \times 2) = 12$ ✓

---

1 Solve algebraically:

$4x - 3y = 8$

$x + y = 9$

2 Solve algebraically:

$y = 2x + 6$

$3y - x = 8$

TEST

Algebra

Inequalities (1)

➤ Q & A

List all the integer values of n that satisfy $-2 \leqslant n < 3$.

Answer

$-2, -1, 0, 1, 2$

Include -2 because the first sign means greater than or equal to -2.

Stop at 2 because the second sign means less than 3.

The four inequality symbols

$<$ means 'less than'.

$\leqslant$ means 'less than or equal to'.

$>$ means 'greater than'.

$\geqslant$ means 'greater than or equal to'.

● Solving an inequality

You solve inequalities in exactly the same way as equations, with one exception: if you multiply or divide by a negative number you must reverse the inequality symbol. This can be tricky, so don't do it! Follow the method below and you'll never have to.

➤ Q & A

Solve $4x + 1 > x - 5$.

Answer

$4x + 1 > x - 5$

$3x + 1 > -5 \qquad [-x]$

$3x > -6 \qquad [-1]$

$x > -2 \qquad [\div 3]$

➤ Method

❶ Get rid of the smallest x-term. This will give you a positive number of x on one side only.

❷ Add/subtract any numbers on the x side to/from both sides.

❸ Divide both sides by the number multiplying x.

● Showing inequalities on a number line

➤ Q & A

Show $-2 < x$ and $0 \leqslant x < 5$ on a number line.

Answer

Shade this circle because the inequality was '$\leqslant$', so 0 is included.

○ means not included

● means is included

Use arrows to show more numbers are included.

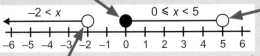

Do not shade as the inequality was '$<$', so 5 is not included.

Do not shade this circle as the inequality was '$<$', so -2 is not included.

38

Algebra

Inequalities (2)

● Showing inequalities on a graph

➤ Q & A

Shade the region on a graph that satisfies $y < x$ and $x \leqslant 5$.

Answer

First, plot the lines $y = x$ and $x = 5$.

Broken lines show points are not included (use if inequality was '<' or '>').

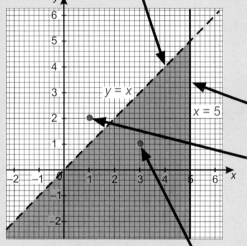

Solid lines show points are included (use for '$\leqslant$' and '$\geqslant$').

Pick a point, e.g. (1, 2), and see if it fits the inequalities:

$2 < 1$ and $2 \leqslant 5$ ✗

(1, 2) does not satisfy $y < x$.

So, pick another point, e.g. (3, 1), and see if it fits the inequalities:

$1 < 3$ and $3 \leqslant 5$ ✓   (3, 1) works, so shade the region it's in.

➤ Method

❶ Replace the inequality symbols with '='.

❷ Draw the lines (plot a table of values or use $y = mx + c$).

❸ Pick a point (not on a line) and if it satisfies the original inequalities shade this region. If not try another point in a different region.

---

1 a List integer values of n that satisfy $-5 < n \leqslant 1$

  b Show the solution to $-5 < n \leqslant 1$ on a number line.

2 a Solve $2x + 2 < x + 4$.

  b Show the solution on a number line.

3 Shade the region on a graph that satisfies $y > -2$ and $y \leqslant 2x$.

4 a Solve $10y - 5 \leqslant 6y + 3$.

  b Show the solution on a graph.

TEST

39

Algebra

Quadratics (1)

● Factorising quadratics

Quadratic expressions are expressions where the highest power is squared.

> ➤ **Examples**
> $x^2 + x + 1$, $3y^2 - 5$

➤ **Q & A**

Factorise $x^2 + 3x - 10$.

Answer

$x^2 + 3x - 10 = (x + ?)(x + ?)$

Factor pairs for -10 are:

1×-10, -1×10, 2×-5 and -2×5

Only $-2 + 5 = 3$, so:

$x^2 + 3x - 10 = (x + {}^-2)(x + 5)$

$= \underline{(x - 2)(x + 5)}$

➤ **Method**

❶ Write out the brackets.

❷ Note down factor pairs of the constant.

❸ Choose the ones that add together to give the number in front of x.

❹ Always multiply out to check your answer.

● 'Difference of two squares'

Quadratics of the form $x^2 - a^2$ always factorise as $(x + a)(x - a)$.

> ➤ **Examples**
> $x^2 - 1 = (x + 1)(x - 1)$
> $x^2 - 9 = (x + 3)(x - 3)$

● Solving quadratic equations algebraically

➤ **Q & A**

Solve $x^2 = 16$.

Answer

$x^2 - 16 = 0$ [-16]

$(x + 4)(x - 4) = 0$ [diff. 2 sq.]

$x + 4 = 0$ gives $\underline{x = -4}$

$x - 4 = 0$ gives $\underline{x = 4}$

➤ **Method**

❶ Move all terms to the left so '= 0' is on the right.

❷ Factorise the quadratic expression.

❸ Put the 1st bracket equal to zero and solve.

❹ Repeat ❸ for 2nd bracket.

---

1 a Factorise $x^2 + 7x + 6$.   **b** Solve $x^2 + 7x + 6 = 0$.

2 a Factorise $x^2 - 2x - 8$.   **b** Solve $x^2 - 2x - 8 = 0$.

3 a Factorise $x^2 - 25$.   **b** Solve $x^2 - 25 = 0$.

TEST

Quadratics (2)

● Quadratic graphs

A quadratic graph is always:
∪-shaped if the number multiplying x^2 is positive
∩-shaped if the number multiplying x^2 is negative.

➤ Q & A

Draw the graph of $y = x^2 + x - 3$.
Answer

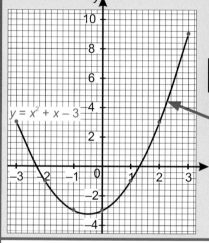

$y = x^2 + x - 3$

➤ Method

❶ Draw a table of values.
❷ Plot the points.
❸ Join the points with a smooth curve.

First draw a table of values:

x	−3	−2	−1	0	1	2	3
$y = x^2 + x - 3$	3	−1	−3	−3	−1	3	9

Draw a smooth curve. Do not draw straight lines between the points.

The graph is ∪-shaped because there is no minus sign in front of x^2.

● Using graphs to solve quadratic equations

To solve $ax^2 + bx + c = 0$, plot $y = ax^2 + bx + c$ and see where $y = 0$ (i.e. where the graph cuts the x-axis).

➤ Q & A

Use the graph above to solve $x^2 + x - 3 = 0$.
Answer

$y = 0$ when $x = -2.3$ and when $x = 1.3$.

By first plotting $y = x^2 - x - 4$, solve $x^2 - x - 4 = 0$.
(Draw your x-axis from −3 to 3 and your y-axis from −6 to 10.)

TEST

41

Algebra

Graphs you should know

You need to be able to <u>recognise</u> all the graphs on this page.
You also need to be able to <u>sketch</u> them from their equations.

● Straight lines

Any graph with equation
$y = mx + c$ is a <u>straight line</u>.

Make sure you can recognise
these special cases:

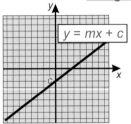

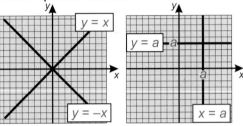

● Quadratics

Any graph with equation
$y = ax^2 + bx + c$ is a
<u>quadratic</u>.
You need to know what
$y = x^2$ and $y = -x^2$ look like.

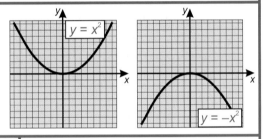

● Cubics

Cubics always have this
basic shape:

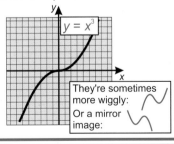

They're sometimes
more wiggly:
Or a mirror
image:

● Reciprocals

Reciprocals (a number over x)
always have this basic shape:

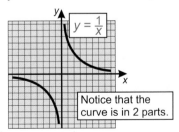

Notice that the
curve is in 2 parts.

Cover the top part of this page. Sketch:

a $y = 3$ **b** $x = -5$ **c** $y = x$ **d** $y = -x$

e $y = x^2$ **f** $y = -x^2$ **g** $y = x^3$ **h** $y = \frac{1}{x}$

TEST

Real-life graphs (1)

● Distance–time graphs

In a <u>distance–time graph</u> the <u>gradient</u> gives the <u>velocity</u> (speed).

➤ Q & A

The graph shows Suki's walk to and from a local shop.

Describe her journey in words.

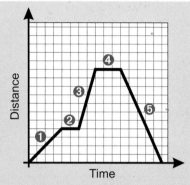

Answer

❶ She starts <u>walking slowly</u>.

❷ She <u>stops</u> for a short while, perhaps because she bumps into a friend.

❸ She starts <u>walking more quickly</u>, perhaps to make up lost time.

❹ She <u>stops</u> in the shop for a while.

❺ She <u>walks home without stopping</u>.

● Velocity–time graphs

In a <u>velocity–time graph</u> the <u>gradient</u> gives the <u>acceleration</u>.

➤ Q & A

The graph shows Mrs Smith's speed as she runs for a bus.

Describe her journey in words.

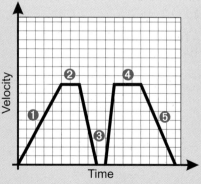

Answer

❶ From a standing start she picks up speed (<u>accelerates</u>).

❷ She then runs at a <u>steady pace</u>.

❸ She <u>slows</u> to a <u>stop</u> then <u>accelerates</u> again, perhaps because she has to cross a road.

❹ She runs at a <u>steady pace</u> again.

❺ She <u>slows down</u> as she approaches the bus stop.

Algebra

Real-life graphs (2)

● Filling bottles with water

> ➤ **Q & A**

Sketch a graph to show the depth of water in this bottle as it is filled.

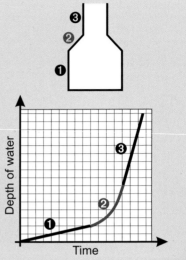

Answer

❶ The bottle is <u>wide</u> at the bottom, so it <u>fills slowly</u> at first.

❷ This part <u>slopes</u>, so the graph will be <u>curved</u>.

❸ The bottle is <u>narrowest</u> here so the graph is <u>steepest</u>.

---

1 The graph shows two trains' journeys. Describe the journeys.

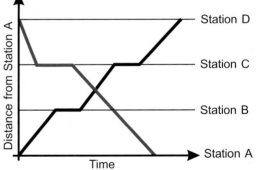

Key:
━━━ Alpha train
━━━ Beta train

2 Sketch graphs to show how the depth of water changes as these bottles are filled.

a   b   c   d

TEST

44

Trial & improvement

● Finding roots

Essential: you must show all your working.

➤ Q & A (1)

Find $\sqrt[3]{12}$ to 1 d.p., using trial and improvement.

Answer

Guess	Cube		
2	8	too small	$\sqrt[3]{12}$ is bigger than 2
3	27	too big	$\sqrt[3]{12}$ is between 2 and 3
2.2	10.648	too small	$\sqrt[3]{12}$ is between 2.2 and 3
2.3	12.167	too big	$\sqrt[3]{12}$ is between 2.2 and 2.3
2.25	11.390 625	too small	$\sqrt[3]{12}$ is between 2.25 and 2.3

As 2.25 and 2.3 both round to 2.3, $\sqrt[3]{12}$ = 2.3 to 1 d.p.

➤ Method

❶ Make a sensible guess at the root.
❷ If this gives an answer too small, then increase your guess. If it's too big, then reduce your guess.
❸ Stop when you have two numbers that bound the answer and round to the same number.

● Solving equations

➤ Q & A (2)

Use trial and improvement to solve $x^3 + x = 100$ to 2 d.p.

Answer

x	$x^3 + x$		
4	68	too small	x is bigger than 4
5	130	too big	x is between 4 and 5
4.5	95.625	too small	x is between 4.5 and 5

Continue to improve this guess in exactly the same way as you did to find $\sqrt[3]{12}$ above (see Test Q2).

➤ Method

❶ Make a sensible guess for x and substitute it into the equation.
❷ If the left-hand side is too big/small, take a smaller/bigger guess.
❸ Stop when you have two numbers that bound x and round to the same number.

---

1 Use trial and improvement to find $\sqrt{30}$ to 3 s.f.
2 Finish **Q & A (2)**.

TEST

Algebra

Sequences

● Linear sequences

The <u>difference</u> between <u>consecutive terms</u> is the <u>same</u>.

➤ Q & A

a What are the next two terms of this sequence?
5, 7, 9, 11, ...

b What is the nth term?

c What is the 100th term?

Answer

a 5   7   9   11   13   15
    +2 +2 +2 +2 +2

b nth term = $2n + 3$

Common difference is <u>2</u>.

First term is $2 + 3 = 5$

> **➤ Method for nth term**
> ❶ Find the <u>common difference</u>, d.
> Write 'nth term = dn'.
> ❷ What do you need to <u>add/subtract</u> to/from d to get the <u>first term</u>? Add/subtract this to dn to complete the <u>nth term</u>.

c Substituting $n = 100$ into nth term: $2 \times 100 + 3 = \underline{203}$

● Quadratic sequences

If the common difference isn't constant, the sequence may be quadratic. This just means it's <u>related to</u> the sequence of square numbers: <u>1, 4, 9, 16, ...</u>

➤ Q & A

Find the nth term of:

a 2, 5, 10, 17, ...

b 2, 8, 18, 32, ...

> **➤ Method**
> ❶ See what you would have to do to <u>each term</u> to get a <u>square number</u>.
> ❷ Do whatever you did to each term to n^2. You have found the <u>nth term</u>.

Answer

a These are the square numbers $\underline{+\ 1}$, so nth term = $\underline{n^2 + 1}$

b These are <u>double</u> the square numbers, so nth term = $\underline{2n^2}$

Find the next term, the nth term and the 100th term:

a 2, 5, 8, 11, ...   **b** 10, 5, 0, –5, ...   **c** 0, 3, 8, 15, ...

TEST

46

Angles & parallel lines

● Angles

Acute angles are between 0° and 90°.

Obtuse angles are between 90° and 180°.

Reflex angles are between 180° and 360°.

Angles on a straight line add up to 180°.

$a + b = 180°$

Angles at a point add up to 360°.

$c + d + e + f = 360°$

Vertically opposite angles are equal.

$p = r$ and $q = s$

● Parallel lines

Alternate angles are equal.

$u = v$

(The angles are in a Z-shape.)

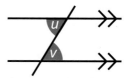

Corresponding angles are equal.

$w = x$

(The angles are in an F-shape.)

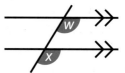

Supplementary angles add up to 180°.

$y + z = 180°$

(The angles are in a C-shape.)

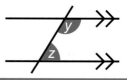

Work out the size of the lettered angles.

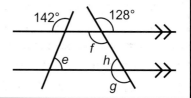

TEST

47

Shape, space & measures

Polygons

- **The angles in a triangle add up to 180°**

  $a + b + c = 180°$

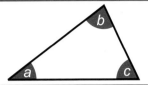

- **The angles in a quadrilateral add up to 360°**

  $w + x + y + z = 360°$

- **Interior and exterior angles**

The angles <u>inside</u> a polygon are called <u>interior angles</u>.

<u>Exterior angles</u> are found on the <u>outside</u> when the <u>sides are extended</u>.

<u>Learn</u> these two formulae:

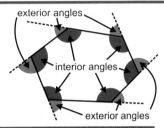

exterior angles

interior angles

exterior angles

> ❶ Sum of exterior angles = 360°
>
> ❷ Sum of interior angles = (number of sides – 2) × 180°

- **Regular polygons**

The <u>sides and angles</u> of a <u>regular polygon</u> are all the <u>same size</u>.

➤ **Q & A**

What is the size of an interior angle in a regular pentagon?

Answer
Using formula ❷ above we get:

Sum of interior angles of a regular pentagon = (5 – 2) × 180° = 540°

There are 5 equal interior angles, so size of one = 540° ÷ 5 = <u>108°</u>

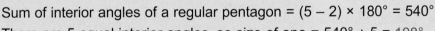

1 Two interior angles of a triangle are 57° and 74°.
   What is the size of the other angle?

2 What are the sizes of the interior and exterior angles of:
   a a square   **b** a regular hexagon   **c** a decagon?

TEST

Perimeter & circumference

● Perimeter

The <u>perimeter</u> is the <u>distance around</u> a <u>2-D shape</u>.

➤ Q & A

What is the perimeter of this shape?

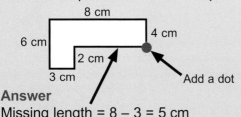

Answer

Missing length = 8 − 3 = 5 cm

Start at the <u>dot</u> and add the sides up clockwise: 5 + 2 + 3 + 6 + 8 + 4 = <u>28 cm</u>

➤ Method

❶ Work out any <u>missing lengths</u>.
❷ Mark a corner with a <u>dot</u>.
❸ Starting at the dot, <u>add</u> the sides as you go around the shape. <u>Stop</u> when you get back to the dot.
❹ <u>Essential</u>: Show your working.

● Circumference of a circle

The <u>perimeter of a circle</u> has a special name: <u>circumference</u>.

> Circumference = π × diameter (*C* = π*d*)

π ≈ 3.14 or 3.142 or press 🟦π (π is a Greek letter, pronounced 'pie'.)

➤ Q & A

This circle has a radius of 5 cm. What is its circumference?

Answer

The <u>radius</u> is 5 cm, so the <u>diameter</u> = 5 cm <u>× 2</u> = 10 cm.

Circumference = π × diameter = 3.14 × 10 = <u>31.4 cm</u>

➤ Method

❶ Find the diameter (<u>the diameter is twice the radius</u>).
❷ Use the formula: *C* = π*d*

---

1 What is the perimeter of an L-shape made by cutting a 2 cm square from the corner of a 3 cm square?

2 What is the circumference/perimeter of a:
  a circle with radius 15 cm   **b** semicircle of radius 4 m?

TEST

Shape, space & measures

Areas of triangles & quadrilaterals

● Area of a triangle

Area = $\frac{1}{2}$ × base × height

$A = \frac{1}{2} \times b \times h$

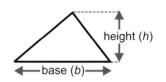

height (*h*)
base (*b*)

● Area of a rectangle

Area = length × width

$A = l \times w$

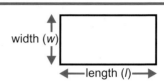

width (*w*)
length (*l*)

● Area of a parallelogram

Area = base × perpendicular height

$A = b \times h$

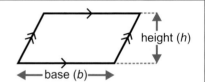

height (*h*)
base (*b*)

● Area of a trapezium

Area = $\frac{1}{2}$ × sum of parallel sides × height between them

$A = \frac{1}{2} \times (a + b) \times h$

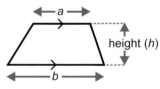

a
height (*h*)
b

> Essential: for triangles, parallelograms and trapeziums make sure that you use the height that's at right angles to the base.

Memorise the formulae above (get someone to test you), then work out the areas of these shapes (remember your units):

a

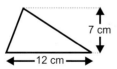

7 cm
12 cm

b

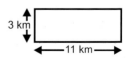

3 km
11 km

c

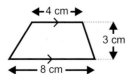

4 cm
3 cm
8 cm

d

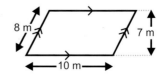

8 m
7 m
10 m

TEST

50

Areas of circles & composite shapes

● Area of a circle

Area = π × radius squared

$$A = \pi r^2$$

Use the **π** button (or π ≈ 3.14 or 3.142).

● Area of composite shapes

➤ Q & A

Work out the area of this shape:

Answer

❶ The shape is a <u>semicircle</u> on top of a <u>triangle</u>.

❷ First, find the area of the semicircle:

Diameter is 6 cm, so the <u>radius is 3 cm</u>.

The <u>area of a circle</u> with radius 3 cm is π × 3² = 3.14 × 9 = 28.26 cm².

So the <u>area of the semicircle</u> is ½ × 28.26 = <u>14.13 cm²</u>.

Next, work out the area of the triangle:

The height of the triangle is 8 − 3 = 5 cm. The base is 6 cm.

So the <u>area of the triangle</u> is ½ × 5 × 6 = <u>15 cm²</u>.

❸ Total area of the shape = 14.13 cm² + 15 cm² = <u>29.13 cm²</u>

➤ Method

❶ Split the shape into <u>simple shapes</u>.

❷ <u>Work out the area</u> of each simple shape.

❸ <u>Add</u> up the areas of the simple shapes to get the <u>total area</u> of the big shape.

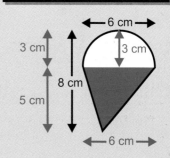

Work out the areas of these shapes:

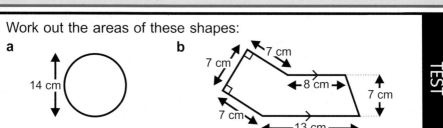

a

b

TEST

Shape, space & measures

Volume & surface area (1)

● Volume of a cuboid

Volume = length × width × height

$V = l \times w \times h$

(This formula works for a
cube, i.e $V = l \times l \times l = l^3$.)

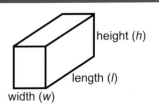

height (*h*)

length (*l*)

width (*w*)

● Volume of a prism

Volume = area of cross-section × length

$V = A \times l$

(A prism is a shape with the same
cross-section all along its length.)

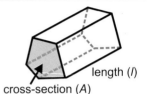

length (*l*)

cross-section (*A*)

➤ Q & A

Work out the volume of
this triangular prism:

Answer

The <u>area</u> of the <u>cross-section</u>
(triangular end) is

$\frac{1}{2} \times 2 \times 5 = 5$ cm^2

The <u>length</u> is 9 cm.

So the <u>volume</u> is

$A \times l = 5 \times 9 = \underline{45 \text{ cm}^3}$

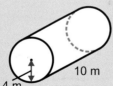

5 cm

9 cm

2 cm

➤ Method

❶ Work out the <u>area</u>
of the <u>cross-section</u>.

❷ Write down the <u>length</u>
of the prism.

❸ Use the formula
$\underline{V = A \times l}$
to work out the volume.

❹ Remember your <u>units</u>
(usually cm^3 or m^3).

➤ Q & A

Work out the
volume of
this cylinder:

Answer

10 m

4 m

The <u>area</u> of the <u>cross-section</u> (circular end) is π × 4^2.

Press 🥧 ✕ 4 x^2 = to get area = 50.27 m^2.

The <u>length</u> is 10 m.

So the <u>volume</u> is $A \times l = 50.27 \times 10 = \underline{502.7 \text{ m}^3}$.

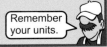

Remember
your units.

Volume & surface area (2)

● Surface area

The surface area of a 3-D shape is the total area of all its faces.

➤ Q & A

Work out the surface area of this triangular prism:

Answer

The area of each triangular end is $\frac{1}{2} \times 3 \times 4 = 6$ cm².

The areas of the rectangular faces are:
$3 \times 6 = 18$ cm²
$4 \times 6 = 24$ cm²
$5 \times 6 = 30$ cm²

➤ Method
❶ Work out the area of each face.
❷ Add the areas together.
❸ Remember your units (usually cm² or m²).

So the total surface area is 6 + 6 + 18 + 24 + 30 = 84 cm².

● Changing units

➤ Q & A

The volume of a cupboard is 4.5 m³. What is the volume in cm³?

Answer

4.5 m³
= 4.5 (100 cm)³   [1 m = 100 cm]
= 4.5 × 100³ cm³
= 4.5 × 1 000 000 cm³
= 4 500 000 cm³

➤ Method
❶ Write the area/volume down.
❷ Write it again with the new length unit in place of the old length unit.
❸ Square (for area) or cube (for volume) the new length unit.
❹ Multiply the numbers.

To go from cm³ to m³, divide by 100³.

---

1 Work out the volume and surface area of these shapes:

a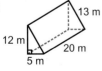

b

c

2 Change the units in your answer in **1a** to cm³ and cm² & **1c** to m³ and m².

TEST

53

Shape, space & measures

Circle theorems (1)

● Chord, tangent & arc

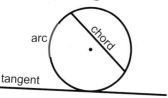

arc

chord

tangent

● Sector & segment

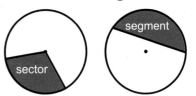

segment

sector

---

❶ Tangent and radius meet at right angles

The <u>tangent</u> at any point on a circle is <u>perpendicular</u> to the <u>radius</u> at that point.

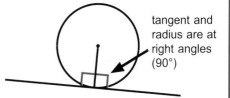

tangent and radius are at right angles (90°)

---

❷ Tangents from an external point are equal in length

PA = PB

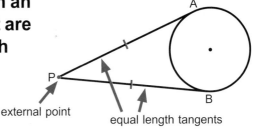

A

P

B

external point

equal length tangents

---

❸ A line drawn from the centre of a circle perpendicular to a chord bisects the chord

AB = BC

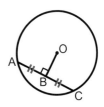

O

A

B

C

---

❹ Angle at circumference of a semicircle is 90°

The angle subtended at the circumference by a semicircle is a right angle.

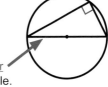

Basically, a <u>triangle</u> drawn from a <u>diameter</u> makes a <u>right angle at the edge</u> of the circle.

Circle theorems (2)

⑤ Angle at centre is twice that at circumference

The <u>angle</u> subtended by an arc at the <u>centre</u> of a circle is <u>twice the angle</u> subtended at any point <u>on the remaining part of the circumference</u>.

⑥ Angles in the same segment are equal

Triangles drawn from a chord have the same angle where they meet the circumference.

The angles have to be on the <u>same side</u> of the chord.

⑦ Opposite angles in a cyclic quadrilateral add up to 180°

$$a + c = 180°$$
$$b + d = 180°$$

A cyclic quadrilateral is a 4-sided shape whose corners are all on the circumference of a circle.

<u>Memorise</u> everything on these two pages, then <u>write down</u> all you can remember.

Then work out the size of:

a angle PRT
b angle ORT

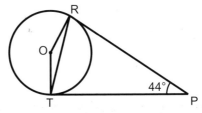

c angle ABC
d angle ADB

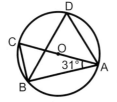

e angle WXY
f angle WZY

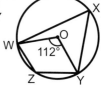

TEST

55

Pythagoras' theorem (1)

- **The square of the hypotenuse is equal to the sum of the squares of the other two sides**

Using letters this is written as:

$$h^2 = a^2 + b^2$$

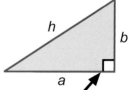

h is the hypotenuse, which is always the longest side (the side opposite the right angle).

Pythagoras' theorem only works in right-angled triangles.

- ## Finding h given a and b

➤ **Q & A**

What is the length of the hypotenuse?

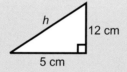

12 cm

5 cm

Answer

From the diagram: $a = 5$, $b = 12$.

$h^2 = 5^2 + 12^2$

$\therefore h^2 = 25 + 144 = 169$

$\therefore h = \sqrt{169}$

$\therefore h = 13$

So the length of the hypotenuse is 13 cm.

➤ **Method**

❶ Write down the values of a and b.

❷ Put these values into $h^2 = a^2 + b^2$.

❸ Find h by solving the equation (take the square root of both sides).

($\therefore$ means 'therefore'.)

- ## Finding b given h and a

➤ **Q & A**

Find the missing length.

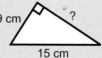

9 cm   ?

15 cm

Answer

From the diagram: $h = 15$, $a = 9$.

$15^2 = 9^2 + b^2$

$\therefore 225 = 81 + b^2$

$\therefore b^2 = 225 - 81 = 144$

$\therefore b = \sqrt{144}$

$\therefore b = 12$, so missing length is 12 cm.

➤ **Method**

❶ Write down the values of h and a (a is always the given side that isn't the hypotenuse).

❷ Put these values into $h^2 = a^2 + b^2$.

❸ Find b by solving the equation.

Pythagoras' theorem (2)

● Finding the distance between two points

➤ Q & A

Work out the distance between the points P(2, 1) and Q(5, 3).

Answer

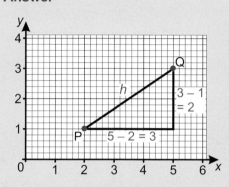

➤ Method

❶ Sketch the two points with a right-angled triangle drawn through them.

❷ Work out the lengths of the horizontal and vertical sides of the triangle (these are your a and b).

❸ Use $h^2 = a^2 + b^2$ to work out the hypotenuse (this is the distance between the two points).

From the diagram: $\underline{a = 3, b = 2}$.

$h^2 = 3^2 + 2^2$ [put values into $h^2 = a^2 + b^2$]

$\therefore h^2 = 9 + 4 = 13$

$\therefore h = \sqrt{13}$

$\therefore h = 3.6$ (to 1 d.p.)

So distance between P and Q is $\underline{3.6\ units}$.

(You can use the $\boxed{\sqrt{\ }}$ button on your calculator to work out square roots.)

---

1 Use Pythagoras' theorem to work out the missing lengths. Give your answers to 1 d.p.

a 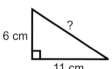 b 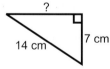 c

2 Work out the distance between these points:
  a (4, 5) and (11, 13)   b (24, 11) and (12, −4)

3 Work out the coordinates of the midpoints of the lines between the points in Q2.
  (Hint: add the x-coordinates then divide by 2, do the same for the y-coordinates.)

TEST

57

Shape, space & measures

Trigonometry (1)

Trigonometry and Pythagoras' theorem both involve <u>right-angled</u> triangles.
The difference is that <u>trigonometry</u> involves <u>angles</u>. <u>Pythagoras'</u> only involves <u>sides</u>.

● Opposite & adjacent (& hypotenuse)

The <u>first thing</u> you should do when faced with a trig question is to <u>label the sides</u> of the triangle in relation to the angle you're interested in:

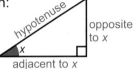
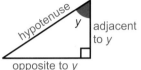

● Sine, cosine & tangent

$$\text{Sin } x = \frac{\text{Opposite}}{\text{Hypotenuse}} = \frac{O}{H}$$

$$\text{Cos } x = \frac{\text{Adjacent}}{\text{Hypotenuse}} = \frac{A}{H}$$

$$\text{Tan } x = \frac{\text{Opposite}}{\text{Adjacent}} = \frac{O}{A}$$

A good way to learn the trig ratios is to <u>remember</u> this 'word':

SOH-CAH-TOA

Or you could make up a phrase to remember like 'Silly Old Harry Caught A Herring Trawling Off America'...

● Finding an angle given two sides

➤ Q & A

Work out the size of angle w.

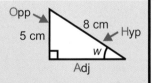

Answer

So Opp = 5 cm and Hyp = 8 cm.

SOH-CAH-TOA tells you that you need to use Sin, so:

$$\text{Sin } w = \frac{\text{Opp}}{\text{Hyp}} = \frac{5}{8} = 0.625$$

Now you have to find the <u>inverse</u>. You should have 0.625 on the screen

(5 ÷ 8), so press [SHIFT] [sin] [=].

This gives <u>$w = 38.7°$</u>.

➤ Method

❶ Label sides Opp, Adj & Hyp in relation to the <u>angle you want</u>.

❷ Write down the two of Opp, Adj & Hyp you have been given.

❸ Use SOH-CAH-TOA to work out whether to use Sin, Cos or Tan.

❹ Find the <u>inverse</u> on your calculator.

Make sure you know how to find the inverse trig functions: $\sin^{-1}$, $\cos^{-1}$ and $\tan^{-1}$ on <u>your</u> calculator.

Trigonometry (2)

● Finding a side given an angle and another side

➤ **Q & A**

Work out the length of side AB.

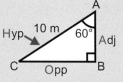

Answer

So Hyp = 10 m, and we need to find AB which is Adj.

SOH-CAH-TOA tells you that you need to use Cos:

$$\text{Cos } 60° = \frac{\text{Adj}}{\text{Hyp}}$$

$$\therefore \text{Cos } 60° = \frac{\text{AB}}{10}$$

$\therefore 10 \times \text{Cos } 60° = \text{AB}$ [×10]

$\therefore \text{AB} = 10 \times \text{Cos } 60°$ [swap sides]

Work this out on your calculator by pressing ① ⓪ ✕ 🄲🄾🅂 ⑥ ⓪ ＝.

This gives an answer of AB = 5 cm.

➤ **Method**

❶ Label sides Opp, Adj & Hyp in relation to the <u>angle you have been given</u>.

❷ Which of Opp, Adj & Hyp have you been given, and which do you have to find?

❸ Use SOH-CAH-TOA to work out whether to use Sin, Cos or Tan.

❹ Form an equation and solve it.

Check this works on <u>your</u> calculator. You may have to press: ① ⓪ ✕ ⑥ ⓪ 🄲🄾🅂 ＝.

● Angle of elevation & depression

Angles of elevation or depression are measured from the horizontal up or down respectively.

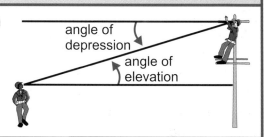

angle of depression

angle of elevation

---

1 Work out the sizes of the lettered angles and sides.

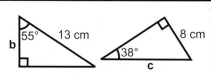

2 Lauren is 28 m from the base of a tree. The angle of elevation from ground level to the top of the tree is 35°. How tall is the tree? (Make a sketch then use trig.)

Shape, space & measures

Bearings

● **Three things you should know about bearings**

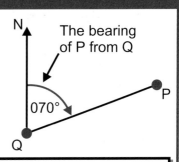

The bearing of P from Q

❶ A bearing is <u>an angle</u> that gives a <u>direction</u>.

❷ Bearings are measured <u>clockwise</u> from the <u>North line</u>.

❸ All bearings are given as <u>3 figures</u>.

➤ **Examples** Look for the word '<u>from</u>'. It tells you where to put the North line (i.e. where to measure <u>from</u>).

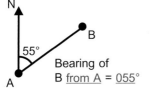

Bearing of B <u>from A</u> = <u>055°</u>

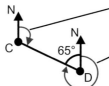

Bearing of D <u>from C</u> = 180° − 65° = <u>115°</u> (supplementary angles)

Bearing of C <u>from D</u> = 360° − 65° = <u>295°</u> (angles round a point)

● **A typical bearings question (with trigonometry)**

➤ **Q & A**

From airport X, a plane flies 130 km East, then 260 km South to airport Y.
What is the bearing of Y from X?

Answer

N
130 km
X a
260 km
Y

Start by working out angle a.

$$\text{Tan } a = \frac{\text{Opp}}{\text{Adj}} = \frac{260}{130} = 2$$

So $a = \text{Tan}^{-1} 2 = 63°$
(Work this out on your calculator.)

Bearing of Y from X
= 90° + 63° = <u>153°</u>

➤ **Method**

❶ Sketch a diagram (including a <u>right-angled triangle</u>).

❷ Use <u>trigonometry</u> to work out the angle or distance you need (see pages 58–59).

❸ Remember to give any bearings with <u>3 figures</u>.

---

1 In the **Q & A** above, what is the bearing of X from Y?

2 A ship sails 58 km due North from point L. It then sails 43 km West to point M. What is the bearing of M from L?

TEST

Plans & elevations

● Drawing plan, front and side elevations

When drawing the plan, front and side elevations (or views) of a 3-D shape, you have to be careful to keep everything in scale.

➤ **Q & A**

On squared paper, draw the plan, front and side elevations of this shape.

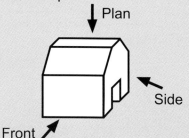

Answer

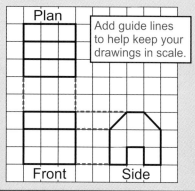

Add guide lines to help keep your drawings in scale.

● Drawing a 3-D shape from elevations

➤ **Q & A**

On isometric paper, draw a 3-D representation from these elevations.

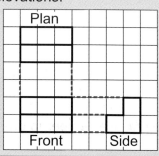

Remember to label the plan, front and side elevations.

Answer

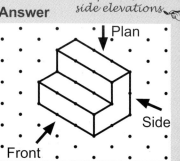

---

1 On squared paper, draw plan, front and side elevations of a square-based pyramid of height 4 cm and base 5 cm.

2 Sketch a 3-D shape that has 4 cm × 2 cm rectangular plan and front views, and a circle of diameter 2 cm for a side view.

TEST

Shape, space & measures

Constructions & loci (1)

● How to construct an equilateral triangle

❶

Draw a line of the length you want the sides to be, e.g. 5 cm.

❷

Set your compasses to 5 cm. Draw two crossing arcs from the ends of the line.

❸

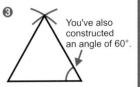

You've also constructed an angle of 60°.

Join the point where the arcs crossed to the ends of the line.

● Perpendicular bisector of a line
Perpendicular means 'at right angles'. Bisect means 'cut in half'.

This is similar to constructing an equilateral triangle.

You just have to draw two more crossing arcs on the other side of the line.

Set your compasses to more than half the length of the line.

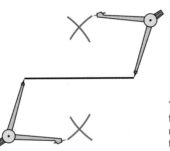

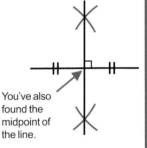

You've also found the midpoint of the line.

● Perpendicular from a point to a line

❶ Draw two arcs on the line, centred on the point. Keep your compasses set at the same distance.

❷ Draw two crossing arcs on the other side of the line, with the compasses centred on the arcs on the line.

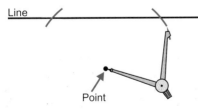

Line

Point

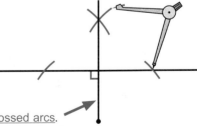

❸ Draw a line from the point to the crossed arcs. This is the perpendicular from the point to the line.

---

1 Construct an equilateral triangle of side 6 cm.
2 Draw a line 8 cm long. Construct its perpendicular bisector.
3 Construct the perpendicular from a point to a line.

TEST

62

Constructions & loci (2)

● Perpendicular from a point on a line

❶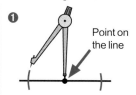
Point on
the line

❷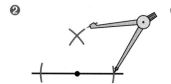

❸

Draw arcs on the line <u>either side</u> of the point. Use the <u>same radius</u>.

<u>Increase</u> the radius. Draw <u>two crossing arcs</u> centred on the arcs on the line.

Join the <u>original point</u> to where the <u>arcs crossed</u>. This is the perpendicular.

● Bisector of an angle

❶

❷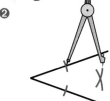

❸
The line cuts the angle in half.

Draw <u>two arcs</u> on the arms of the angle, <u>centred on the vertex</u>.

Draw <u>two crossing arcs</u> inside the angle, <u>centred on the arcs</u> on the arms.

Join the <u>vertex</u> to the point where the <u>arcs crossed</u>.

● Loci

A <u>locus</u> is a <u>set of points</u> (often lines) that <u>satisfy a given rule</u>.
Here are <u>four loci</u> that you should <u>know</u> (loci are in colour):

❶

❷

❸

❹

A fixed distance from a point is a circle.

A fixed distance from a straight line is two parallel straight lines.

Equidistant from two points is the perpendular bisector of the line joining the two points.

Equidistant from two straight lines is the bisectors of the angles between the lines.

Types ❶ & ❷ are often combined:

Fixed distance from a line segment

---

1 Construct a perpendicular 5 cm from the end of a 14 cm line.
2 Draw a 68° angle with a protractor. Bisect it with compasses.
3 Construct the locus of points 4 cm from a line 6 cm long.

TEST

Shape, space & measures

Congruent & similar shapes

● Similar shapes

Similar shapes are exactly the same shape.

Congruent shapes are exactly the same shape *and* size.

➤ Q & A

Which of these are similar, congruent or neither?

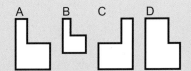

Answer

A and C are similar to B. A is congruent to C. D is neither.

● Similar shapes are enlargements of each other

➤ Q & A

These two triangles are similar. Calculate the missing lengths.

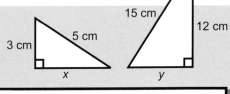

Answer

Use the hypotenuses to find the scale factor.

$$5 \text{ cm} \xrightarrow{\times 3} 15 \text{ cm}$$

So the s.f. is 3.

y is the shortest side so it corresponds to 3 cm:

$y = 3 \text{ cm} \times 3 = \underline{9 \text{ cm}}$ ◄———

That leaves x and 12 cm:

$x = 12 \text{ cm} \div 3 = \underline{4 \text{ cm}}$ ◄———

➤ Method

❶ Use the common length to find the scale factor (s.f.) that takes you from the small triangle to the large one.

❷ Multiply/divide by the s.f. to find the missing lengths.

Multiply when you are going from the small triangle to the large one.

Divide when going from large to small.

---

1 Are these similar, congruent or neither?

a A and B **b** A and C

2 D is similar to B. Find x.

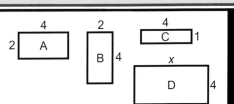

TEST

64

Symmetry

● Reflection symmetry in 2-D shapes

Often called <u>line symmetry</u> because you draw <u>lines of symmetry</u> (mirror lines) which divide the shape in half.

➤ Q & A

Draw all the lines of symmetry on each of these shapes.

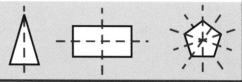

● Reflection symmetry in 3-D shapes

Often called <u>plane symmetry</u> because you draw <u>planes of symmetry</u>.

➤ Q & A
Draw a cube, cone and an isosceles triangular prism. Indicate one plane of symmetry in each.

Answer

All these shapes have more than one plane of symmetry. See TEST Q2.

● Rotation symmetry

The <u>order of rotation symmetry</u> is the number of times a shape fits exactly over itself during a full-turn about its centre.

➤ Q & A

What is the order of rotation symmetry of these shapes?

<u>4</u>   <u>3</u>   <u>1</u>

Note: Order of rotation symmetry 1 means <u>no rotation symmetry</u>.

TEST

1 Draw an equilateral triangle, a square and a regular hexagon.
  a Draw all the lines of symmetry on each shape.
  b Write down the order of rotation symmetry for each shape.
  c What do you notice?
2 Copy the cube, cone and isosceles triangular prism above. Draw a different plane of symmetry on each.

Shape, space & measures

Transformations (1)

A <u>transformation</u> maps the <u>object</u> (original shape) to an <u>image</u> (a new shape in a different position).

● Translation

A <u>translation</u> is defined by a <u>distance</u> and a <u>direction</u>.

A <u>vector</u> can be used to show the distance and direction.

➤ Q & A

a Describe the translation that takes A to B.

b Translate A by $\begin{bmatrix} -2 \\ -4 \end{bmatrix}$. Label the new shape A_1.

Answer

a A needs to move 6 left, 1 up to get to B. As a vector that's: $\begin{bmatrix} -6 \\ 1 \end{bmatrix}$

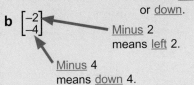

Use a <u>minus</u> to show moves <u>left</u> or <u>down</u>.

b $\begin{bmatrix} -2 \\ -4 \end{bmatrix}$

Minus 2 means <u>left</u> 2.

Minus 4 means <u>down</u> 4.

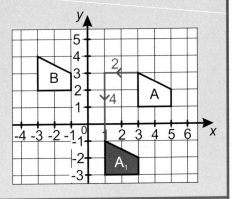

● Reflection   A <u>reflection</u> is defined by a <u>mirror line</u>.

➤ Q & A

Reflect A in the line $x = 1$.
Label the new shape A_2.

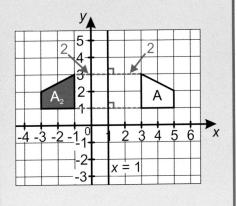

➤ Method

❶ Draw the <u>mirror line</u>.

❷ Draw lines from the corners of A to the mirror line <u>at right angles</u>.

❸ Draw the corners of A_2 the <u>same distance</u> from the mirror line.

Transformations (2)

● Rotation

A <u>rotation</u> is defined by its <u>centre</u> and an <u>anticlockwise angle</u>.

These can be quite hard, so always use tracing paper to help you.

➤ Q & A

a Rotate A through 90° about (3, 3). Label the new shape A_3.

b Describe the rotation that takes A to C.

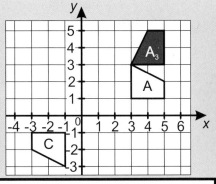

Answer

a

> ### ➤ Method for a
> ❶ <u>Trace</u> shape A.
> ❷ Put the point of your pencil on the centre of rotation and <u>rotate A anticlockwise</u> through the given angle.
> ❸ Draw and label A_3.

b Rotation through 180° about (1, 0)

> ### ➤ Method for b
> ❶ <u>Guess</u> the centre of rotation.
> ❷ Use tracing paper and the method for **a** to <u>see if you are right</u>.
> ❸ If not, <u>keep guessing</u>. (Your guesses will improve with practice.)

---

1 Describe the transformation from P to

a Q **b** R **c** S.

2 Copy the axes and shape Q.

a Translate Q by $\begin{bmatrix} 5 \\ -2 \end{bmatrix}$.

b Reflect Q in $y = x + 1$.

c Rotate Q through 90° about (−1, 0).

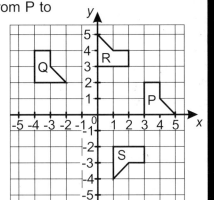

TEST

67

Shape, space & measures

Transformations (3)

● Enlargement

An <u>enlargement</u> is defined by its <u>centre</u> and a <u>scale factor</u>.

➤ Q & A

a Enlarge A by a scale factor of 2 about (–1, 1). Label the image B.

b C is an enlargement of D. Describe the enlargement.

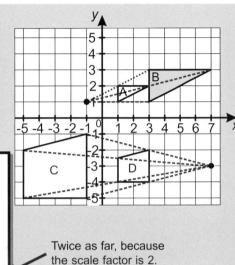

Answer

a

> **➤ Method for a**
>
> ❶ <u>Draw 'rays'</u> from the centre of enlargement through the vertices of A.
>
> ❷ Draw the vertices of A′ on these rays, <u>twice as far</u> from the centre.

Twice as far, because the scale factor is 2.

b Enlargement with scale factor $\frac{1}{2}$, centre (7, –3)

The scale factor is a fraction because the image is smaller than the object.

> **➤ Method for b**
>
> ❶ <u>Draw 'rays'</u> through corresponding vertices. The point where these cross is the <u>centre</u>.
>
> ❷ Measure <u>corresponding lengths</u> to find the scale factor.

---

1 Draw axes with both *x* and *y* from –10 to 10.

  a Plot these points. Join them in order. Label the shape A.
    (–5, –1), (–7, –5), (–5, –3), (–1, –5), (–5, –1)

  b Enlarge A using:
    i centre (–7, –9), s.f. 2   **ii** centre (–7, –9), s.f. $\frac{1}{2}$

2 Look again at the **Q & A**.
  Describe the transformation from **a** B to A **b** D to C.

Dimensions

● Length, area or volume?

The <u>dimensions</u> of a formula are the <u>number of lengths multiplied together</u> in each term.

❶ <u>Length</u> has <u>1 dimension</u>.

❷ <u>Area</u> terms are always <u>length × length</u>, so area has <u>2 dimensions</u>.

❸ <u>Volume</u> terms are always <u>length × length × length</u>, so volume has <u>3 dimensions</u>.

> ### ➤ Example

❶ l, w and h are lengths.

❷ hw, lw and hl are all areas (of faces).

❸ lwh is the volume.

➤ Q & A

p, q and r are all lengths.

Decide whether each expression is a length, area, volume or none of these.

➤ Method

❶ <u>Look at the first term</u>. Is it length, length × length or length × length × length? (Remember: length^2 means length × length.)

❷ <u>Check the other terms</u> are the same. If an expression is, e.g. length + area, it isn't a length or an area.

Answer

Expression	Type
$p + q$	<u>Length (2 terms, both lengths)</u>
3	<u>None (numbers have no dimensions)</u>
$10pq$	<u>Area (ignore any numbers multiplying lengths)</u>
$p + 2r$	<u>Length</u>
$8pr^2$	<u>Volume</u>
$q^2 + r^2$	<u>Area</u>
$pq + 5r$	<u>None (area + length)</u>
$pqr + p^3$	<u>Volume</u>

I've just come from another dimension.

Are these lengths, areas or volumes? (All letters are lengths.)

a $10a^2$ **b** $xyz + 2$ **c** $pq + qr + rs$ **d** π **e** $3u + 5t$ **f** $c^2d + cd^2$

TEST

Shape, space & measures

Rounding measures

● Accuracy of measurement

Measurements are often given to the <u>nearest whole unit</u>.
The measurement could really be up to <u>half a unit more or less</u> than the given value.

> ### ➤ Example
>
> 17.5 cm, 17.9 cm, 18.2 cm and 18.4 cm all round to 18 cm to the nearest centimetre.
>
> The <u>smallest number</u> that rounds to 18 cm is 17.5 cm.
> The <u>largest number</u> that rounds to 18 cm is really 18.4999... cm, but this is a bit long-winded so we call it 18.5 cm.
>
> So <u>18 cm to the nearest cm</u> could be anything from <u>17.5 cm to 18.5 cm</u>.

➤ Q & A

The weight of a bag of seed is given as 2.7 kg to the nearest 100 g.

What are the upper and lower bounds for the weight of the bag?

Answer

➤ Method

❶ Decide what units to work in.
❷ <u>Check what accuracy</u> the measurement is given to.
❸ <u>Add half of this</u> to the measurement to find the <u>upper bound</u>.
❹ <u>Subtract half</u> from the measurement to find the <u>lower bound</u>.

In this case it's easiest to work in grams, then convert back to kilograms at the end.

2.7 kg is 2700 g   100 g ÷ 2 = 50 g

Upper bound = 2700 g + 50 g = 2750 g = <u>2.75 kg</u>
Lower bound = 2700 g − 50 g = 2650 g = <u>2.65 kg</u>

---

1 Measurements are given to the accuracy shown in brackets. Write down the maximum and minimum values.

    a 43 hours (nearest hour)   **b** 27 pints (nearest pint)

    c 2.8 cm (nearest mm)   **d** 9.2 litres (nearest 100 ml)

TEST

Shape, space & measures

Converting between measures

Learn all the conversions on this page. Go on, test yourself.

● Metric units

Length: 1 km = 1000 m, 1 m = 100 cm, 1 cm = 10 mm
Mass: 1 tonne = 1000 kg, 1 kg = 1000 g
Capacity: 1 litre = 1000 ml, 1 litre = 100 cl, 1 cl = 10 ml, 1 ml = 1 cm³

● Imperial units

Length: 1 yard (yd) = 3 feet (ft), 1 foot (ft) = 12 inches (in)
Mass: 1 stone (st) = 14 pounds (lb), 1 pound (lb) = 16 ounces (oz)
Capacity: 1 gallon (gal) = 8 pints (pt)

● Metric to imperial

Length: 8 km ≈ 5 miles, 1 m ≈ 39 in, 30 cm ≈ 1 ft, 2.5 cm ≈ 1 in
Mass: 1 kg ≈ 2.2 lb, 25 g ≈ 1 oz
Capacity: 1 litre ≈ 1.75 pt, 4.5 litres ≈ 1 gal

➤ Q & A
a What is 1200 m in km?
b What is 20 km in miles?
Answer
a 1000 m = 1 km   [fact]
 1 m = 0.001 km   [÷1000]
 1200 m = 1.2 km   [×1200]
b 8 km ≈ 5 miles   [fact]
 1 km = 0.625 miles [÷8]
 20 km = 12.5 miles [×20]

➤ Method
❶ <u>Write down</u> the most suitable <u>conversion fact</u> you know.
❷ Use it to find <u>one unit</u>.
❸ <u>Multiply</u> to find the number of units required.

1 Convert **a** 3 st to pounds (imperial) **b** 35 cl to litres (metric).
2 Convert between metric and imperial:
   a 45 cm to feet   **b** 20 gallons to litres

TEST

71

Compound measures

- **Speed =** $\dfrac{\text{Distance}}{\text{Time}}$

There are 3 ways of writing this formula:

$$S = \frac{D}{T} \qquad T = \frac{D}{S} \qquad D = S \times T$$

All 3 ways can be remembered using this 'formula triangle':

➤ Q & A

A car travels at 70 mph for 2.5 hours. How far does it go?

Answer

Distance is needed so cover up D.

This gives D = S × T

D = 70 × 2.5 = 175

The car travels 175 miles.

➤ Method

❶ Cover up what you want on the formula triangle. Write down the formula this gives.

❷ Write the formula with the numbers you know. (Make sure the units match. e.g. if the speed has hours in it, the time must be in hours.)

❸ Solve to find the unknown.

- **Density =** $\dfrac{\text{Mass}}{\text{Volume}}$

Like the one for speed, this formula can also be written in a 'formula triangle':

➤ Q & A

A block has a density of 22 kg/m³. The mass of the block is 88 kg. What is the volume of the block?

Answer

Volume is needed so cover up V.

This gives V = $\frac{M}{D}$

So V = $\frac{88}{22}$ = 4

The block has a volume of 4 m³.

---

1 How long will a car travelling at 60 km/h take to travel 40 km?

2 Calculate the mass of 2 m³ of wood of density 500 kg/m³.

TEST

Mode, median, mean, range

➤ **Q & A** (see below for answers)

Find the mode, median, mean and range of this set of data:

110, 155, 145, 120, 125, 160, 125, 140, 115, 155

● Mode

The mode is the most common value.
If there are two most common values there are two modes.

Putting the data in order makes it easier to spot the mode:

110, 115, 120, 125, 125, 140, 145, 155, 155, 160

125 and 155 are the modes because they both occur twice.

● Median

The median is the middle value when the values are written in order.
If there is an even number of values, the median is halfway between
the middle two.

110, 115, 120, 125, 125, 140, 145, 155, 155, 160

There are ten values, so the median is halfway between the middle two.

Median = (125 + 140) ÷ 2 = 132.5

● Mean

The mean is the sum of the values divided by the number of values.

110 + 115 + 120 + 125 + 125 + 140 + 145 + 155 + 155 + 160 = 1350

Mean = 1350 ÷ 10 = 135

When most people talk about 'the average' they're usually referring to 'the mean'.
But be careful, because the median and mode are also 'averages'.

● Range

The range is the difference between the highest and lowest values.

110, 115, 120, 125, 125, 140, 145, 155, 155, 160

Range = 160 – 110 = 50

Find the mode, median, mean and range of this set of data:
0.7, 1.2, 1.5, 1.2, 1.2, 1.6, 1.0, 0.8, 0.7

TEST

Handling data

Time series & moving averages

● Time series graphs

➤ **Q & A** This table shows a household's quarterly gas bills.

Year	1999				2000				2001			
Quarter	Q1	Q2	Q3	Q4	Q1	Q2	Q3	Q4	Q1	Q2	Q3	Q4
Charge (£)	85	45	55	79	96	47	58	83	94	52	59	89

a Plot the data as a time series. **b** Comment on the graph.
c Plot the 4-point moving average. **d** Comment on the trend.

Answer

a

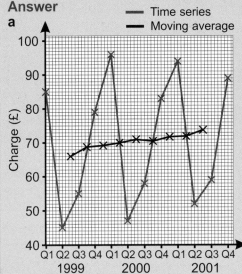

— Time series
— Moving average

➤ **Method for 4-point moving average** (M.A.)
❶ Find the <u>mean of the 1st to 4th</u> values.
❷ Find the <u>mean of the 2nd to 5th</u> values.
❸ Continue finding the means, <u>moving on one quarter at a time</u>.
❹ Plot each mean in the <u>middle of the 4 points</u> used.

b High charges in Q1 and Q4 reflect colder months.
c 1st M.A. = (85 + 45 + 55 + 79) ÷ 4 = 66
   2nd M.A. = (45 + 55 + 79 + 96) ÷ 4 = 68.75
   Remaining M.A.s: 69.25, 70, 71, 70.5, 71.75, 72, 73.5
d The charges are slowly increasing.

---

1 Check the moving averages then re-plot the graph.
2 Use the seasonal variation to estimate the charge for Q1 of 2002. Plot this on the same graph.
3 Use your point to calculate then plot the next moving average.
4 Does your estimate fit the trend?

TEST

74

Frequency tables

● Two-way tables

Two-way tables help you get more out of your data.

➤ Q & A

A group of friends own 60 DVDs and videos between them.
The girls own 18 of the DVDs.
The boys own 9 of the 40 videos.
How many DVDs do the boys own?

Answer

	DVDs	Videos	Total
Boys own	2	9	11
Girls own	18	31	49
Total	20	40	60

Start here:
9 + ? = 40

The boys own 2 DVDs.

➤ Method

❶ Put the information you know into a table.
❷ Look for rows/columns with one missing entry.
❸ Use known values to find missing values.
❹ Read off the answer.

● Averages

➤ Q & A

Find the mean number of cars per household.

Answer

No. of cars	Frequency	Freq. × No. of cars
0	6	0
1	11	11
2	29	58
3	4	12
Totals	50	81

Mean = 81 ÷ 50 = 1.62 cars

➤ Method

❶ Multiply each value by its frequency.
❷ Total these products.
❸ Divide by the total frequency.

Add an extra column to the table to record the 'Frequency × No. of cars'.

---

1 Repeat the first **Q & A** with boys owning 19 videos.

2 What is the median number of cars per household?
(The median is the middle value. Its position is found by adding 1 to the total frequency then dividing by 2.)

3 What is the modal number of cars? (Look for highest frequency.)

TEST

Handling data

Grouped frequency tables

● Estimating the mean from grouped data

You don't have the raw data, so you can only estimate the mean.

➤ Q & A

The table shows the lengths of candles on a birthday cake.
Estimate the mean length.

➤ Method

❶ Add a column of midpoints.
❷ Multiply each midpoint by its frequency.
❸ Total this column.
❹ Divide by the total frequency.

Answer

Length (L mm)	Frequency	Midpoint	Freq. × midpoint
$80 \leqslant L < 90$	2	85	170
$90 \leqslant L < 100$	2	95	190
$100 \leqslant L < 110$	3	105	315
$110 \leqslant L < 120$	6	115	690
$120 \leqslant L < 130$	3	125	375
Total	16	Total	1740

Estimated mean = 1740 ÷ 16 = 109 mm (to nearest mm)

● Median

You can't give an exact value for the median, but you can say which group it's in.

➤ The median is the 8.5th value, which is in the $110 \leqslant L < 120$ group.

● Modal group

The modal group has the highest frequency.

➤ The modal group is $110 \leqslant L < 120$.

These are the heights (h cm) of 20 students:
152, 167, 169, 158, 177, 165, 172, 168, 156, 161,
163, 166, 171, 157, 162, 169, 168, 155, 176, 167

a Put the data into a frequency table with groups
$150 \leqslant h < 155$, $155 \leqslant h < 160$, ... (Use tallies to help you.)
b Use the table to calculate an estimate for the mean.
c Which group is the median in? **d** Which is the modal group?

TEST

Frequency diagrams

● Bar charts and histograms

Bar charts are used to show discrete data. The bars do not touch.
Histograms show grouped continuous data. The bars touch.

➤ Q & A

Draw a histogram to show the candle length data on page 76.

Answer   It's a histogram, not a bar chart, so make sure the bars touch.

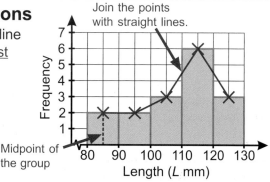

➤ Method

❶ Make sure the data is grouped in equal class widths.

❷ Evenly space the group boundaries along the horizontal axis.

❸ Label the vertical axis 'Frequency'.

❹ Draw a bar for each group. Its height is the frequency.

● Frequency polygons

A frequency polygon is a line graph of frequency against midpoint.

Joining the tops of the histogram bars is the easiest way to draw a frequency polygon.

Join the points with straight lines.

Midpoint of the group

---

1 Draw a histogram for the height data in the TEST on page 76.

2 Join the tops of the bars to make a frequency polygon.

3 On a new sheet of graph paper, try drawing the frequency polygon without using histogram bars to help you. (Plot frequencies against midpoints.) Check by comparing with **2**.

TEST

Handling data

Stem & leaf diagrams

A stem and leaf diagram is like a bar chart or histogram, but each bar is made up of the actual data.

▶ Q & A

These are the interest rates (%) offered on 20 bank accounts.

0.5, 2.4, 3.2, 3.1, 1.2, 4.0, 3.0, 1.5, 2.5, 4.5,
1.0, 1.0, 3.5, 2.8, 2.6, 1.0, 2.9, 0.5, 4.3, 2.0

a Show the data on a stem and leaf diagram.

b Find the mode and median.

Answer

a The 'stem' is just the first part of the number, in this case units. The 'leaf' is the rest of the number, in this case tenths.

0	5 5
1	2 5 0 0 0
2	4 5 8 6 9 0
3	2 1 0 5
4	0 5 3

Stem = units, leaves = tenths

Reorder the leaves in a 2nd table.

0	5 5
1	0 0 0 2 5
2	0 4 5 6 8 9
3	0 1 2 5
4	0 3 5

Stem = units, leaves = tenths

▶ Method

❶ Look at the numbers in the list. Use the first one or two digits to make the 'stem'.

❷ Go back through the list, crossing the numbers off one at a time and adding them to the diagram.

❸ When all the numbers are on the diagram, redraw it with the leaves in each row ordered from smallest to largest.

b Mode = 1.0 (there are three of these)

The median is the $\frac{20 + 1}{2}$ = 10.5th value, which is halfway between 2.5 and 2.6.

Median = (2.5 + 2.6) ÷ 2 = 2.55

---

30 students got these marks in a test.

50, 75, 51, 68, 72, 48, 62, 58, 65, 62, 42, 70, 54, 67, 60,
73, 74, 69, 62, 59, 63, 72, 62, 63, 57, 69, 49, 56, 58, 70

a Draw the stem & leaf diagram. **b** Find the mode and median.

TEST

Pie charts

● Drawing pie charts

➤ Q & A (1)

Draw a pie chart for this shopping budget.

Food	£31
Drinks	£12
Personal hygiene	£8
Cleaning products	£6
Other	£3

➤ Method
❶ Add up the amounts.
❷ Calculate $360° ÷ ❶$.
❸ Multiply each amount by ❷.
❹ Check the angles add to 360°.
❺ Draw and label the sectors.

Answer
The total price is £60.
$360 ÷ 60 = 6$

Item	Price	Angle
Food	£31	31 × 6 = 186°
Drinks	£12	12 × 6 = 72°
Personal hygiene	£8	8 × 6 = 48°
Cleaning products	£6	6 × 6 = 36°
Other	£3	3 × 6 = 18°
Total	£60	360°

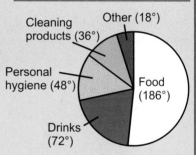

Tip: when using a 180° protractor, it is often easier to draw the small angles first.

● Reading pie charts

➤ Q & A (2)

Out of 30 pupils, how many watched BBC?

Answer

The BBC sector is 120°.

It is $\frac{120°}{360°} = \frac{1}{3}$ of the chart.

$\frac{1}{3}$ of 30 = $\frac{1}{3}$ × 30 = 10 pupils watched BBC.

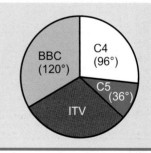

1 Show these tie colours on a pie chart.
   Red 40%, Blue 35%, Green 15%, Other 10%
2 Look at **Q & A (2)**. How many watched the other channels?

TEST

79

Handling data

Cumulative frequency (1)

The <u>cumulative frequency</u> (C.F.) is the <u>running total</u> of frequency up to the <u>end of the group</u>. You always plot it at the <u>end of the group</u>.

➤ Q & A

These are the weights of wheelie bins in a street.

Weight (W kg)	Frequency
$0 \leqslant W < 5$	5
$5 \leqslant W < 10$	12
$10 \leqslant W < 15$	27
$15 \leqslant W < 20$	14
$20 \leqslant W < 25$	2

Draw a cumulative frequency graph.

Answer

Add a 3rd column to the table to work out the C.F.s:

Cumulative frequency
5
5 + 12 = 17
17 + 27 = 44
44 + 14 = 58
58 + 2 = 60

Think of cumulative frequency as the 'running total'.

➤ Method

❶ Calculate the <u>C.F.s</u>.
❷ Draw a <u>horizontal axis</u> for the <u>end-points</u> of the groups. Draw a <u>vertical axis</u> for <u>C.F.</u>
❸ Plot each <u>C.F.</u> against the group <u>end-point</u>.
❹ Join the points with a <u>smooth curve</u>.

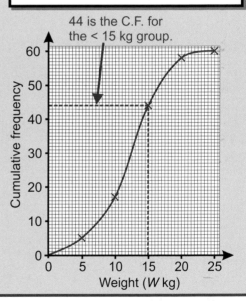

44 is the C.F. for the < 15 kg group.

● Reading from the graph

You can use the graph to find out how many wheelie bins weigh more or less than a particular weight.

➤ Example

The C.F. for 18 kg is 54. This means that 54 bins weigh up to 18 kg.

Check this on the graph by drawing a line up from 18 kg to the curve. Then draw a line across to the cumulative frequency axis. Go on!

Cumulative frequency (2)

● Median, quartiles & interquartile range

The median is halfway through the distribution.

The lower quartile (LQ) is a quarter of the way through.

The upper quartile (UQ) is three-quarters of the way through.

> Interquartile range (IQR) = upper quartile − lower quartile

➤ Q & A

Use the cumulative frequency graph to find

a the median

b the interquartile range.

Answer

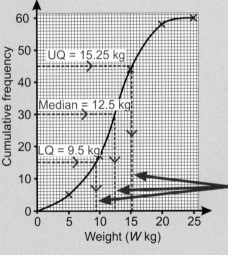

➤ Method

❶ Decide how far up the C.F. axis you need to go: halfway for the median, a quarter of the way for the LQ, three-quarters of the way for the UQ.

❷ Draw a horizontal line to the C.F. curve.

❸ Draw a vertical line down to the other axis.

❹ Read off the value.

The total C.F. is 60, so the median has C.F. = 60 ÷ 2 = 30, the LQ has C.F. = 60 ÷ 4 = 15, the UQ has C.F. = 60 ÷ 4 × 3 = 45.

Now, read off the values for the median, UQ and LQ from the graph.

a Median = 12.5 kg   b IQR = UQ − LQ = 15.25 − 9.5 = 5.75 kg

Plot the cumulative frequency curve for these TV prices. Use it to find the median, lower and upper quartiles, and the interquartile range.

TV price (£P)	150–	200–	250–	300–	350–
Frequency	3	8	12	6	1

TEST

81

Handling data

Box plots

Box plots (or box and whisker diagrams) are used to compare data.

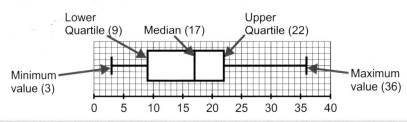

Lower Quartile (9) Median (17) Upper Quartile (22)

Minimum value (3) Maximum value (36)

➤ Q & A
Show the information given in this table on a box plot.

	Min	Max	LQ	UQ	Median
Weight (kg)	4	37	7	33	24

Answer

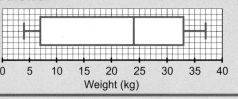

Weight (kg)

➤ Method
❶ Draw and label a horizontal axis.
❷ Draw a box from LQ to UQ.
❸ Mark the median.
❹ Draw whiskers from min to max.

➤ Q & A
Compare this box plot with the one above.

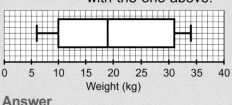

Weight (kg)

➤ Method
❶ Look at the medians and say which data is bigger on average.
❷ Look at the range and IQR to see which data is more spread out.

Answer

Weights are higher on average in the first plot (higher median).

The range (min to max) and interquartile range (LQ to UQ) are bigger in the first plot, so these data are more spread out.

Look at this box plot. Write down the min, max, LQ, UQ and median.

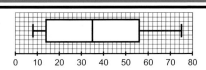

TEST

Scatter graphs

Scatter graphs show whether two sets of data are related.

➤ Q & A

Here are some students' results for two maths tests.

Test 1	11	18	14	12	16	11	17	18	13	15
Test 2	10	17	11	11	13	8	16	15	9	13

a Draw a scatter graph of the data.   **b** Draw a line of best fit.

Answer

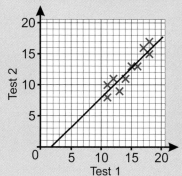

➤ **Method for b**

❶ Decide if the line should <u>slope up or down</u>.

❷ Carefully draw the line with <u>half the points above it</u>. (It doesn't have to go through the origin.)

● **Correlation**

Decide whether the <u>points are roughly in a line</u>, and, if you can, <u>how close</u> they are to the line.

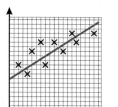

Positive correlation (⟋)
<u>Strong</u> if the points are all <u>close to the line</u>, otherwise <u>weak</u>.

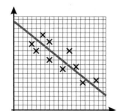

Negative correlation (⟍)
<u>Strong</u> if the points are all <u>close to the line</u>, otherwise <u>weak</u>.

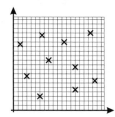

No linear correlation
The points may be related, but <u>not</u> <u>linearly</u>.

---

1 What type of correlation do the points in the **Q & A** show?

2 Repeat the **Q & A** for these test results.

English	19	5	12	12	14	18	10	8	13	17
ICT	18	8	14	11	17	15	8	12	10	13

3 Predict the ICT result for someone who got 15 in English.

TEST

Handling data

Probability (1)

Probabilities can be given as fractions or decimals, but they are always between 0 and 1. If something has probability 0 it can't happen; if it has probability 1 it will definitely happen.

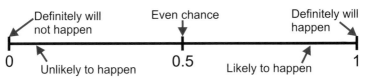

Definitely will not happen

Even chance

Definitely will happen

0   Unlikely to happen   0.5   Likely to happen   1

● Calculating probabilities

Theoretical probability = $\dfrac{\text{Number of successful outcomes}}{\text{Total number of possible outcomes}}$

➤ Q & A

You roll a fair dice. What is the probability of getting:

a 6   **b** an even number?

Answer

6 possible outcomes: 1, 2, 3, 4, 5, 6

a 1 successful outcome: 6
$P(6) = \frac{1}{6}$

b 3 successful outcomes: 2, 4, 6
$P(\text{even}) = \frac{3}{6} = \frac{1}{2}$

➤ Method

❶ List the possible outcomes.
❷ Pick out the 'successful outcomes'.
❸ Calculate the theoretical probability.
❹ Simplify if possible.

P(6) is a short way of writing 'the probability of getting 6'.

● Mutually exclusive

Outcomes are mutually exclusive if they can't happen at the same time.

The probabilities of all mutually exclusive events add up to 1.

Something will always 'happen' or 'not happen' so

P(happen) + P(not happen) = 1 &

P(not happen) = 1 – P(happen).

➤ Example

You can't get a head *and* a tail when you toss a coin.

➤ Example

When you roll a dice:
$P(6) = \frac{1}{6}$ so
$P(\text{not }6) = 1 - \frac{1}{6} = \frac{5}{6}$

Probability (2)

● Tree diagrams

If you <u>roll a dice twice</u>, the number you get the first time <u>doesn't affect</u> the number you get the second time.

Events like this are called <u>independent events</u>.

Outcomes of independent events can be shown on <u>tree diagrams</u>.

➤ Example

Tossing a coin twice:

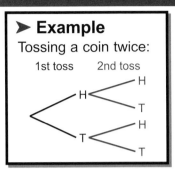

● Experimental probability

You can carry out trials to estimate probability, e.g. rolling a dice lots of times.

$$\text{Estimated probability} = \frac{\text{Number of successful trials}}{\text{Total number of trials}}$$

The more trials, the better the estimate.

➤ Q & A

Here are the results of rolling a dice 100 times.

Number	1	2	3	4	5	6
Frequency	16	17	20	13	15	19

Estimate the probability of getting a 5.

Answer

$P(5) = \frac{15}{100} = \frac{3}{20}$

➤ Method

❶ Use the <u>formula</u> to calculate the probability.

❷ <u>Simplify</u> if possible.

---

1 What is the probability of picking a Queen from an ordinary pack of playing cards?

2 A bag contains 3 red, 4 blue and 1 yellow bead.
   a What is the probability of picking a red bead?
   b What is the probability of *not* picking a yellow bead?

3 You roll a dice twice to try to get a 6. Show the outcomes on a tree diagram. (Be careful: each roll has *two* outcomes.)

4 Look at the last **Q & A**. Estimate the probabilities of the other outcomes.

TEST

85

Revision TEST

These questions test the basic facts. The simple truth is that the more of them you can answer, the better you'll do in your exams. So try them as often as you can. (The answers can be found on the pages given at the end of each question.)

1 When you multiply/divide a number by 10/100, what happens to the digits? (p4)
2 What is the easy way to multiply by 11? (p4)
3 What do even numbers end in? What do odd numbers end in? (p5)
4 What are the first five square, cube and triangular numbers? (p5)
5 What is any non-zero number to the power of zero? (p6)
6 What is any number to the power of one? (p6)
7 What is six to the power of minus one? (p6)
8 What are the missing words? (p7)
   To multiply powers of the same number you _____ the indices.
   To divide powers of the same number you _____ the indices.
   To take the power of a power you _____ the indices.
9 What is a multiple? What is a factor? (p8)
10 How do you find the LCM of two numbers? What about the HCF? (p9)
11 What are the first seven prime numbers? (p10)
12 What is 60 expressed as a product of its prime factors? (p11)
13 When adding or subtracting fractions, what must be the same? (p12)
14 How do you divide a fraction by a fraction? (p13)
15 How do you convert a fraction to a decimal? (p14)
16 What are the eight decimal equivalents you should know? (p14)
17 What does the fraction button look like on your calculator? (p14)
18 How can you tell if a fraction will give a terminating decimal? (p15)
19 What is the short way of writing one-third as a recurring decimal? (p15)
20 What does 'per cent' mean? (p15)
21 How do you convert a percentage to a fraction? to a decimal? (p15)
22 How do you convert a decimal to a percentage? (p16)
23 How do you convert a fraction to a percentage? (p16)
24 Many percentage problems can be solved by first finding what? (p17)
25 What is the formula for 'Percentage change'? (p18)
26 Write the ratio 175 : 250 in its simplest form. (p19)
27 What are the two rules for multiplying and dividing negative numbers? (p21)
28 Round 24.9374 to 2 decimal places. (p23)
29 Round 0.07457 to 2 significant figures. (p23)
30 Work out **a** $(6 \times 10^5) \times (2 \times 10^4)$ **b** $(2.5 \times 10^5) + (3.4 \times 10^4)$ (p25–26)
31 What does the standard form button look like on your calculator? (p26)
32 What does BIDMAS stand for? (p27)
33 Explain what these are: term, expression, equation, formula. (p28)
34 What does 'collect like terms' mean? (p30)
35 When multiplying out double brackets, what should you draw? (p31)
36 What does 'factorising' mean? (p31)
37 What does 'making x the subject of a formula' mean? (p32)
38 How do you work out the gradient of a line? (p34)

Revision TEST (2)

39 How do you know if the gradient is positive or negative? (p34)

40 In '$y = mx + c$', what do m and c tell you? (p35)

41 Why is there no excuse for getting simultaneous equations wrong? (p36)

42 What are the four inequality symbols, and what do they mean? (p38)

43 When showing inequalities on a number line, what do ○ and ● mean? (p38)

44 When showing inequalities on a graph, what does a broken line mean? (p39)

45 What is the highest power in a quadratic expression? Factorise $x^2 - a^2$. (p40)

46 Sketch: **a** $x = -4$ **b** $y = x$ **c** $y = -x$ **d** $y = x^2$ **e** $y = -x^2$ **f** $y = x^3$ **g** $y = \frac{1}{x}$ (p42)

47 What does the gradient give in a distance–time graph? velocity–time? (p43)

48 What should you do first when answering a trial & improvement question? (p45)

49 The difference between consecutive terms in a linear sequence is what? (p46)

50 What do the angles on a straight line add up to? angles at a point? (p47)

51 Sketch diagrams to show: **a** vertically opposite angles **b** alternate angles **c** corresponding angles **d** supplementary angles. (p47)

52 What do the angles in a triangle add up to? What about a quadrilateral? (p48)

53 What are the two formulae concerning interior and exterior angles? (p48)

54 What is special about a *regular* polygon? (p48)

55 What is the formula for the circumference of a circle? What is π? (p49)

56 Give the formulae for the area of a triangle, rectangle, parallelogram, trapezium, and a circle. (p50–51)

57 What is the formula for the volume of a cuboid? What about a prism? (p52)

58 Draw a circle and label these: chord, tangent, arc, sector, segment. (p54)

59 Write down the seven circle theorems, including diagrams. (p54–55)

60 What is Pythagoras' theorem? (p56)

61 What are the formulae for sin, cos and tan? (p58)

62 What are the three things you should know about bearings? (p60)

63 What are the four loci that you should know? Draw accurate diagrams. (p63)

64 Similar shapes are what? Congruent shapes are what? (p64)

65 How many lines of symmetry does a pentagon have? (p65)

66 What is the order of rotation symmetry of a square? (p65)

67 How are these defined: translation, reflection, rotation, enlargement? (p66–68)

68 Give the metric to imperial conversions for length, mass and capacity. (p71)

69 Sketch the formula triangles for speed and density. (p72)

70 How do you work out the mode, median, mean and range? (p73)

71 How do you find the mean from a frequency table? (p75)

72 How do you estimate the mean from a grouped frequency table? (p76)

73 The group with the highest frequency is called what? (p76)

74 Joining the middle of the tops of the bars in a histogram gives what? (p77)

75 How do you work out the interquartile range? (p81)

76 What are the five things that a box plot shows? (p82)

77 Draw diagrams to show positive, negative and no correlation. (p83)

78 What is the probability of something impossible/certain happening? (p84)

79 What is the formula used to work out theoretical probability? (p84)

80 What is the formula used to work out estimated probability? (p85)

Answers

Page 4 Non-calculator tricks
1 **a** 562 181.3 **b** 56 218 130 **c** 562 181 300
2 **a** 30.0218 **b** 0.030 021 8
3 **a** 1169 **b** 1900 **c** 120 **d** 1.6 **e** 3080

Page 5 Special numbers
1 **a** 2, 4, 6, 8, 10, 12, 14, 16, 18, 20
   b 1, 3, 5, 7, 9, 11, 13, 15, 17, 19
   c 1, 4, 9, 16, 25, 36, 49, 64, 81, 100
   d 1, 8, 27, 64, 125, 216, 343, 512, 729, 1000
   e 1, 3, 6, 10, 15, 21, 28, 36, 45, 55
2 **a** 108, 36, 10, 64 **b** 81, 97, 21
   c 81, 36, 64 **d** 64 **e** 10, 21, 36

Page 7 Powers & roots (2)
1 **a** 144 **b** 64 **c** 32 **d** 1 **e** 100 **f** $\frac{1}{100}$ = 0.01
2 **a** 6 **b** 8 **c** 10 **d** 7 **e** 3
3 **a** 7^7 **b** 2^5 **c** 5^{24}

Page 8 Multiples & factors
1 **a** 7, 14, 21, 28, 35
   b 12, 24, 36, 48, 60
   c 21, 42, 63, 84, 105
   d 104, 208, 312, 416, 520
2 **a** 1, 2, 3, 4, 6, 8, 12, 24
   b 1, 2, 4, 7, 8, 14, 28, 56
   c 1, 2, 7, 14, 49, 98

Page 9 LCM & HCF
1 **a** 24 **b** 144 2 **a** 4 **b** 7

Page 10 Prime numbers
1 2, 3, 5, 7, 11, 13, 17, 19, 23, 29, 31, 37, 41, 43, 47
2 **a** No **b** No (both are multiples of 2)
   c No (multiple of 5)
3 All are multiples of 3, so not prime

Page 11 Prime factorisation
1 **a** 114 **b** 468 **c** 4347
2 **a** 2^6 **b** 3^4 **c** $2^3 \times 3 \times 19$ **d** $5^2 \times 7^2$
   e $2 \times 3 \times 5 \times 7 \times 11$

Page 13 Fractions (2)
1 **a** $\frac{7}{8}$ **b** $\frac{1}{3}$ **c** $1\frac{1}{12}$ 2 **a** $\frac{5}{28}$ **b** $1\frac{3}{5}$ **c** $6\frac{1}{9}$

Page 14 Fractions (3)
1 **a** 0.02 **b** 0.375 **c** 2.68
2 See answers to page 13

Page 16 Fractions, decimals & percentages (2)
1 Yes (20 = $2^2 \times 5$)
2 **a** 0.6̇ **b** 0.3̇6̇ **c** 0.1̇42857̇
3 **a** $\frac{3}{4}$ **b** $\frac{3}{8}$ **c** $1\frac{1}{10}$ 4 **a** 0.55 **b** 0.175 **c** 1.3

Page 18 Percentages (2)
1 **a** 37.5 g **b** 212.5 g 2 £20
3 Price without VAT is £80 4 12.5%

Page 19 Percentages (3) (TEST on p20)
£70 246.40

Page 20 Ratio & proportion (2)
1 **a** 1 : 6 **b** 9 : 5 **c** 3 : 8 2 35 : 43
3 240 ml : 560 ml 4 £6.75

Page 21 Negative numbers
a −4 **b** 30 **c** −144 **d** −3 **e** −26 **f** 20

Page 23 Rounding (2)
1 27 900, 2900, 100 2 0.58, 0.02, 12.88
3 350, 1.0, 0.81 4 **a** 5 **b** 1000

Page 24 Standard index form (1)
a 3.45×10^2 **b** 2.4×10^{-4} **c** 4.5×10^4
d 7.64×10^8 **e** 2.453×10^{-6} **f** 1.0×10^7

Page 25 Standard index form (2)
1 **a** 3700 **b** 0.000 44 **c** 5 430 000
   d 0.000 001 2

Page 26 Standard index form (3)
1 **a** 2×10^{10} **b** 8.2×10^7 **c** 2×10^3
   d 2×10 **e** 2.4×10^5 **f** 7.64×10^4
   g 4×10^{-3} **h** 8.13×10^7

Page 27 BIDMAS & bracket buttons
a 198 **b** 169 **c** $\frac{5}{7}$ **d** 176

Page 28 Using letters
1 **a** Term (or single-term expression)
   b Expression **c** Formula **d** Equation
2 **a** 1.5p **b** C = 10 − 1.5p

Page 29 Substituting values
1 £320 2 **a** 13 **b** −16 3 **a** 15 **b** 30 **c** 25

Page 30 Simplifying expressions (1)
1 **a** 6a **b** $3x^2 + 5x$
2 **a** 9x − 19y **b** $p^2 − 2p + 4$

Page 31 Simplifying expressions (2) & Factorising expressions
1 **a** $x^2 + 9x + 20$ **b** $2x^2 − 4x − 6$
   c $4y^2 − 18y + 18$
2 **a** 2(3y − 1) **b** 5(2p + 1) **c** r(s + 1)
3 **a** 2y(9y − 2) **b** $p^2(p + 1)$ **c** s(12r^2 + 3r − 4)
4 $\frac{5}{x}$

Page 32 Rearranging formulae
1 **a** $q = \frac{\sqrt{p}}{2}$ **b** $q = \frac{\sqrt{p}}{9}$

5 **a** 75% **b** 5% **c** 140%
6 135%, $3\frac{1}{4}$, 345%, 4.6

TEST answers

2 a $a = 1 - 3b$ **b** $a = 2b$

Page 33 Solving equations
1 $g = 1$
2 $y = 3$
3 $p = -11$
4 **a** $m = 8$ **b** $n = 4$

Page 35 Straight line graphs (2)
1

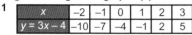

x	−2	−1	0	1	2	3
$y = 3x - 4$	−10	−7	−4	−1	2	5

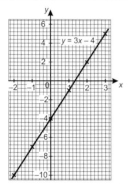

Cuts x-axis at $(1.3, 0)$

2 **a** Gradient = 3, cuts y-axis at $(0, 5)$
   b Gradient = 2, cuts y-axis at $(0, -1)$
3 **a** $y = 2x$ **b** $y = -2x + 6$ **c** $y = x + 2$

Page 36 Simultaneous equations (1)
1 $x = 4, y = 1$
2 $x = 1, y = -1$
3 Their graphs are parallel, so they do not cross

Page 37 Simultaneous equations (2)
1 $x = 5, y = 4$
2 $x = -2, y = 2$

Pages 39 Inequalities (2)
1 **a** −4, −3, −2, −1, 0, 1
   b

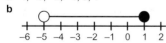

2 **a** $x < 2$
   b

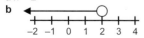

3

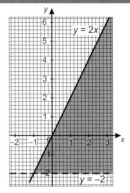

4 **a** $y \leqslant 2$
   b

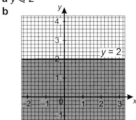

Page 40 Quadratics (1)
1 **a** $(x + 1)(x + 6)$ **b** $x = -1$ or -6
2 **a** $(x + 2)(x - 4)$ **b** $x = -2$ or 4
3 **a** $(x + 5)(x - 5)$ **b** $x = -5$ or 5

Page 41 Quadratics (2)

x	−3	−2	−1	0	1	2	3
$y = x^2 - x - 4$	8	2	−2	−4	−4	−2	2

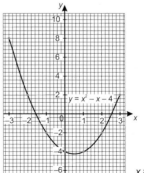

$x = -1.6$ or 2.6

Answers

Page 42 Graphs you should know

a–d

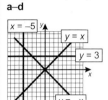

e–f

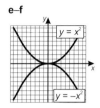

g

h

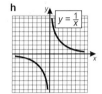

Page 44 Real-life graphs (2)

1 Alpha train travels at a steady speed from A to D, stopping at stations B and C.
   Beta train travels quickly from D to C, where it stops, then travels to A without stopping at B. The trains pass each other between B and C.

2 a   b

2 c   d

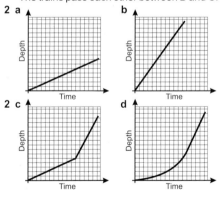

Page 45 Trial & improvement

1 5.48 (use your calculator to check)
2 $x = 4.57$

Page 46 Sequences

a 14, $3n - 1$, 299 **b** -10, $15 - 5n$, -485
c 24, $n^2 - 1$, 9999

Page 47 Angles & parallel lines

$a = 65°$, $b = 56°$, $c = 124°$, $d = 124°$,
$e = 38°$, $f = 128°$, $g = 128°$, $h = 52°$

Page 48 Polygons

1 $49°$ ($180° - 57° - 74°$)
2 **a** Interior = 90°, Exterior = 90°
   b Interior = 120°, Exterior = 60°
   c Interior = 144°, Exterior = 36°

Page 49 Perimeter & circumference

1 12 cm   2 **a** 94.2 cm **b** 20.6 cm

Page 50 Areas of triangles & quadrilaterals

a 42 cm² **b** 33 km² **c** 18 cm² **d** 70 m²

Page 51 Areas of circles & composite shapes

a 153.9 cm² **b** 122.5 cm² (square + trapezium)

Page 53 Volume & surface area (2)

1 **a** 600 m³, 660 m² **b** 126 m³, 152.4 m²
   c 2261.9 cm³, 980.2 cm² (curved surface is a rectangle, width same as circumference)
2 **a** 6×10^8 cm³, 6.6×10^6 cm²
   c 0.002 261 9 m³, 0.098 02 m²

Page 55 Circle theorems (2)

a 68° (isosceles triangle)
b 22° (tangent and radius at right angles)
c 90° (angle at circumference of semicircle)
d 59° (angles in same segment)
e 56° (angles at centre and circumference)
f 124° (cyclic quadrilateral)

Page 57 Pythagoras' theorem (2)

1 **a** 12.5 cm **b** 12.1 cm **c** 19.6 km
2 **a** 10.6 units **b** 19.2 units
3 **a** (7.5, 9) **b** (18, 3.5)

Page 59 Trigonometry (2)

1 **a** 31.0° (tan) **b** 7.5 cm (cos) **c** 13 cm (sin)
2 19.6 m (tan)

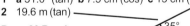

Page 60 Bearings

1 333°
2 323° (use tan, subtract from 360°)

Page 61 Plans & elevations

1

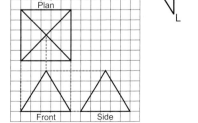

TEST answers

2

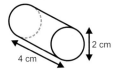

2 cm

4 cm

Page 62 Constructions & loci (1)
1 Check sides are 6 cm, angles are 60°
2 Check your line is 4 cm from each end and at right angles
3 Check lines are at right angles

Page 63 Constructions & loci (2)
1 Check lines are at right angles
2 Check the two parts of the angle are 34°
3

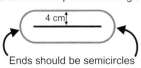

4 cm

Ends should be semicircles

Page 64 Congruent & similar shapes
1 **a** Congruent **b** Neither
2 $x = 8$ (s.f. is 2)

Page 65 Symmetry
1 **a**

b 3, 4, 6
c No. of lines of symmetry = order of rotational symmetry = no. of sides (true for all regular polygons)
2 Make sure the halves are mirror images

Page 67 Transformations (2)
1 **a** Translation $\begin{bmatrix} -7 \\ 2 \end{bmatrix}$
b Reflection in the line $y = x$
c Rotation of 270° about (1, 0)
2

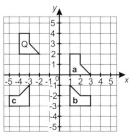

Page 68 Transformations (3)
1

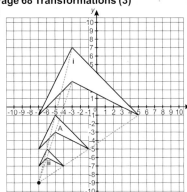

2 **a** Enlargement with centre (–1, 1), s.f. $\frac{1}{2}$
b Enlargement with centre (7, –3), s.f. 2

Page 69 Dimensions
a Area **b** None (volume + number) **c** Area
d None (π is a number) **e** Length **f** Volume

Page 70 Rounding measures
1 **a** Max = 43.5 hours, Min = 42.5 hours
b Max = 27.5 pints, Min = 26.5 pints
c Max = 2.85 cm, Min = 2.75 cm
d Max = 9.25 litres, Min = 9.15 litres

Page 71 Converting between measures
1 **a** 42 lb **b** 0.35 litres
2 **a** About 1.5 ft **b** About 90 litres

Page 72 Compound measures
1 40 minutes
2 1000 kg

Page 73 Mode, median, mean, range
Mode = 1.2, Median = 5th ordered value = 1.2,
Mean = 9.9 ÷ 9 = 1.1, Range = 1.6 – 0.7 = 0.9

Page 74 Time series & moving averages
2 About £98 seems reasonable
3 Using £98, the next M.A. is 74.5
4 Check trend line continues to go up slowly

Page 75 Frequency tables
1 The boys still own own 2 DVDs
2 2 cars (25.5th value)
3 2 cars

Answers

Page 76 Grouped frequency tables

a

Height (h cm)	Tally	Frequency
150 ≤ h < 155	I	1
155 ≤ h < 160	IIII	4
160 ≤ h < 165	III	3
165 ≤ h < 170	ЖІ III	8
170 ≤ h < 175	II	2
175 ≤ h < 180	II	2

b 3310 ÷ 20 = 165.5 cm (midpoints: 152.5, etc)
c 165 ≤ h < 170 d 165 ≤ h < 170

Page 77 Frequency diagrams

1

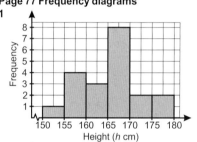

3

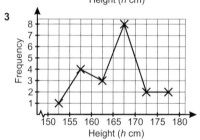

Page 78 Stem & leaf diagrams

a
```
40 | 2 8 9
50 | 0 1 4 6 7 8 8 9
60 | 0 2 2 2 2 3 3 5 7 8 9 9
70 | 0 0 2 2 3 4 5
```
Stem = tens, leaves = units

b Mode = 62, Median = 62 (15.5th value)

Page 79 Pie charts

1

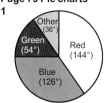

2 ITV: 9 pupils
C4: 8 pupils
C5: 3 pupils

Page 81 Cumulative frequency (2)

TV price (£P)	Frequency	Cumulative freq.
150–	3	3
200–	8	11
250–	12	23
300–	6	29
350–	1	30

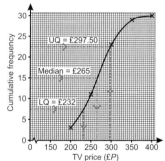

Median = £265, LQ = £232, UQ = £297.50
Interquartile range = £297.50 − £232 = £65.50

Page 82 Box plots

Minimum = 8, Maximum = 75
LQ = 14, UQ = 56, Median = 35

Page 83 Scatter graphs

1 Strong positive correlation
2

3 About 14 (using line of best fit)

Page 85 Probability (2)

1 $\frac{4}{52} = \frac{1}{13}$ 2 a $\frac{3}{8}$ b $\frac{7}{8}$

3

1st roll   2nd roll

```
          6  ──── 6
        ╱    ──── Not 6
      ╱
      ╲
        ╲  ──── 6
        Not 6
             ──── Not 6
```

4 $P(1) = \frac{16}{100} = \frac{4}{25}$ $P(2) = \frac{17}{100}$
$P(3) = \frac{20}{100} = \frac{1}{5}$ $P(4) = \frac{13}{100}$ $P(6) = \frac{19}{100}$

Index

Index

Index

Index